CONQUERING BUSYNESS

CONQUERING BUSYNESS

A proven plan to get more done without adding more, grinding more or hustling more.

Kathy Bourque

Copyright © 2019 Kathy Bourque

All rights reserved. No part of this publication may be reproduced, distributed, or transmitted in any form or by any means, including photocopying, recording, or other electronic or mechanical methods, without the prior written permission of the publisher, except in the case of brief quotations embodied in reviews and certain other non-commercial uses permitted by copyright law.

This is a work of nonfiction. Nonetheless, the names, personal characteristics of individuals, and details of events have been changed in order to disguise identities or protect the privacy of the author's clients and students. Any resulting resemblance to persons living or dead is entirely coincidental and unintentional. The author of this book does not dispense medical advice or prescribe the use of any technique, either directly or indirectly, as a form of treatment for physical, emotional, or medical problems, without the advice of a physician. The author's intent is only to offer information of a general nature to help you in your quest for emotional, physical and spiritual well-being. In the event you use any of the information in this book, the author and the publisher assume no responsibility for your actions.

ISBN: 9781797676289

Dedication

To all of the middle management people out there, whether you are a director, a manager, a coordinator, or a shift boss; for you are the linchpins of every organization.

Acknowledgements

To my family, friends and mentors who make up my entire support system. I am eternally grateful for your wisdom, insight and more importantly, giving me great times to practice what I teach.

GRAB YOUR FREE GIFTS!

In my experience, the best way to get the most out of a non-fiction book is to implement and take action as you go.

To help with this, you'll find a ton of resources mentioned throughout this book that can all be accessed on the resources page.

You can also grab a free copy of the complimentary workbook here:
www.kathybourque.com/busyness-workbook

Table of Contents

Dedication v
Grab Your Free Gifts! vi
Introduction ix

Chapter One
The education that matters most - soft skills. 1

Chapter Two
You are a leader. 7

Chapter Three
Creating your life with intention. 11

Chapter Four
Priorities aren't enough. 15

Chapter Five
Why should anyone want to be led by you? 21

Chapter Six
The battle cry for whitespace. 27

Chapter Seven
The simplicity of one thought. 33

Chapter Eight
Values - Let your soul speak 39

Chapter Nine
Labels - What's in a name? 57

Chapter Ten
Blinded by the Light - Becoming Aware 67

Chapter Eleven

RElabeling - Who do you love? 75

Chapter Twelve

Mindfulness & Choosing a new response 83

Chapter Thirteen

Mindset & Why training is important 95

Chapter Fourteen

That's not me 105

Chapter Fifteen

TIP: Give yourself a break 113

Chapter Sixteen

TIP: The Excuse Clause 117

Chapter Seventeen

TIP: Learning to see other people's perspectives 119

Chapter Eighteen

TIP: New habits, New responses 121

Chapter Nineteen

TIP: Show up and go bold 127

References 129

Introduction

Any idiot can face a crisis. It is the day to day living that wears you out.

~ unknown

It was the fall of 2010. As a *seasoned* owner of a UPS Store (I had been in business for 14 years after-all), I was returning from our national conference buzzing with energy. I had so many important initiatives to get back and implement!

There was the customer recognition campaign that I knew was going to increase my loyalty rates. There was the new commercial series with the catchy song, "Don't you worry about a thing" that they were rolling out. (Finally! We all know how a catchy commercial can make or break a business!) And I couldn't forget to order the new counter displays they had shown plus implement the printing solutions website and …

"Kathy, thank *God* you are back. The copier is doing that jamming thing again and we have an order that has to be out the door in 20 minutes!"

"Kathy, Brianna is going to be late, Timmy was sick and she had to go get him from school. She may not be able to make it in at all. Can you believe she is doing that again?"

"Kathy, the radio guy is out front waiting to see you and oh, by the way, the toilet is backed up for some reason."

"Boss, that customer from last week is on the phone and he is not happy! He says Rachel was rude to him."

"Kathy, we need you now!"

This was not the first time all of my big ideas got put on the back burner. Heck, I was lucky that they didn't fly right on out the window. There were times I couldn't even remember why I had thought going into business for myself was even a good idea. When I could remember the reasons and what ignited my passions, I found that they would only carry me for a couple of days. Soon, I was getting sucked back down into the minutia and the problems and the constant never-ending drama that came with running a business that had started to feel a whole lot like a daycare.

I am guessing you bought this book for one of a dozen or more reasons, maybe even similar to some of those that I was experiencing.

In today's crazy busy world, it is so easy to become overwhelmed. We are under a constant barrage of texts, tweets, emails, calls, IMs, pop-up alerts, bells, whistles, dings and dongs. If you work in healthcare, as I now do, the barrage can feel even more intense. In an industry where regulations and reimbursements create shifting sand under your feet, workforce issues create real challenges and the inner politics make you understand why there was a soap opera named *General Hospital*, the day-to-day business can wear a person out.

It can be easy to find yourself feeling as if you are spinning your wheels. In a workplace where you are running around constantly putting out fires, day in and day out. Where you can't help but asking, "Why is this happening to me?"

But the fact that you are reading this right now is a sign.

Let me ask you something. Do you set goals but never have time to complete them because you get drug into conversations that seem to feed off of drama? Do you find yourself in meetings that seem to have no purpose or find yourself taking on additional responsibility constantly? Do you shelve all your big ideas to the back burner until soon they are forgotten? Until one day you read an article (or worse yet, the CEO brings up the subject you have shelved for the umpteenth time) and it's like "oh yeah, I need to work on that"?

Do your people seem to need you for every little decision? Do they lack ownership and accountability? Do at times you feel like you are running an adult daycare?

If so, you are not alone. Not by a long shot. At the time of this writing there are over 50,000 productivity books on Amazon alone. This doesn't even begin to cover the workshops, conferences and seminars that cover the subject.

Being productive is great, but being *effective* is better. Think of it like this: productivity = generic no-name ice cream while effectiveness = Ben & Jerry's. Yes, it's that good.

As a leader, I know it is seductive to get pulled into the tail-chasing, high-inducing, never-ending cycle of addiction that comes with feeling needed and working all of the time. But this is where burnout happens. It is also where busyness lives. If you are like many leaders I know, there are probably more times than not that you find yourself burning the candle at both ends; answering email at 10:00 p.m. on a Sunday evening, going into work an hour and half early, or working through lunch at your computer.

But there is a better way.

Take a moment to imagine it for yourself.

Imagine getting everything you need to get done during 40 hours a week instead of 65.

Imagine your team taking ownership and working without constant input from you. Imagine feeling less stressed and frazzled. ***This is what being effective feels like.***

As a mentor of mine once said, **"Busyness is an epidemic. Effectiveness is the cure."**

At the time, I was an entrepreneur who felt overwhelmed by the constant barrage of daily fires that seemed to crop up in my small six-person business.

There were days I truly wanted to change my name. At the very least, I wanted to change my position. I dreamed of working at Walmart as the greeter. Ahhhh - that would be true bliss for at least an hour, just smiling, welcoming people, lining up carts. Admit it, you've had this dream too, haven't you?

Busyness had become my Achilles heel.

I was so busy running on the hamster wheel of management that I couldn't put any energy into being a leader. What was worse, I felt so overwhelmed that I was constantly thinking faster than my mouth could talk. It got to the point where I gave my staff permission to grab me by the ears when they were answering a question I had just asked them. This was because my mind had moved on and I hadn't heard the answer.

Yes, I was distracted most of the time. Not only did this distraction cause countless errors, but it also came off as rude, uncaring and selfish. This was not the kind of person I wanted to be nor the energy I wanted to put out in the world.

The truth of the matter is that busyness can be hurting you in ways you may not even fathom. For starters, it may be feeding further overwhelm in your team. When you send emails at 10:00 p.m. on a Sunday night, the people on your team may feel like they are behind the 8-ball when they get to work on Monday morning. I realize this may mean that you feel ready to tackle the week first thing on Monday, but for your team it can be overwhelming. Soon they will start to abandon ship or raise a mutiny in order to get you to slow down.

What's more, when they see you work like this, they realize that they want more to life than working late and coming in early, and therefore a succession plan may be impossible to create.

That's why I'm writing this book. Not only for me, to get these ideas out of my head, but also for you. Mainly for you. You see, I struggled with 'Busyness' for years. Around 20 to be exact. And I still find myself being sucked in by that old familiar foe from time to time. I have come to realize that this isn't just a small business epidemic, it happens in large organizations too.

I have been on a journey leading me to effectiveness and it has made all of the difference in my life, not to mention my sanity.

This book is about cutting out the 20 years of constantly trying to do more with less time. It is about helping you avoid the missteps and giving you the tools, tips and tricks that I use to help me feel more in control of my day.

To get stuff done.

Done without the drama. Done without the overload. Done in balance with who you are and what you want to do in your life.

To be effective.

There are many traditional leadership resources available that speak to the processes of great leadership. These are amazing places to start. Take for instance how we currently develop our leaders. In healthcare, every educational opportunity seems to need CEUs (continuing education credits) and have concrete takeaways.

Because of this, we tend to make everything too technical, too formal and well - too bookish. This works when teaching processes.

However, that is the exact reason this method sets managers and leaders up for failure. Leadership is not a process.

In the leadership development courses I have taken including my masters' degree and the leadership development institute through a hospital association, the technical aspects of leadership were covered.

In my own institution, we teach about the different departments and the big leadership ideas like change management, team building, hiring staff and the like. I am not knocking these, as they are very important parts of managing. But they don't begin to scratch the surface of how to become an effective leader.

What we are missing is the lessons about managing our minds and ditching the emotional drama that seems to encircle us human beings. This book addresses the human aspects of leadership because learning those are what will help you stop the busyness cycle and start moving down the path to becoming more effective.

So, this isn't a book about if you are a transactional leader or a transformational one. We are not going to cover roles or theories of leadership. It does not teach process.

Instead we are going to cover how you can be the best leader *you* can be. In a way that serves you and how you want to show up. In a way that makes your life feel easier, in balance *and* more productive.

This book is for you if are ready to try something new. But I want to give you a word of caution. The word is *awareness*. Because once you see something, you can't unsee it. The thing you will be seeing is yourself, how your mind works and how your reactions and habits are either serving you or challenging you.

I am going to ask you to dig deep. This is a working book. The main requirement is time. Time to think and ask yourself questions in order to know yourself and what thoughts will serve you.

While I don't recommend it if you are looking for a quick fix, there are tips at the end that can be digested in small bite-sized pieces. However, I want to challenge you to give yourself the gift of working on you. There is nothing more valuable to your leadership journey than that.

Enjoy.

Chapter One

The education that matters most - soft skills.

If you think your problem is from out there, you'll try to solve it from outside. Take the shortcut: solve it from within.

~ Byron Katie.

We live in a world where more is better. We are constantly trying to do more, be more, have more. For many of us, working longer hours than anyone else has become a badge of honor. We are in a race to see who is the busiest. We are martyrs if we come in early, stay late and work through lunch.

We answer the famous,

"How have you been?" question with

"Busy". (Smiley-face.)

"And you?"

"Oh, the same."

All of this busyness is creating burnout in mass proportions. In their 2018 report, Gallup found that 67% of employees report feeling burned out some of the time, if not all of the time[1]. People and

---

[1] Gallup, Inc. (2018). State of the American Workplace. Retrieved from *https://news.gallup.com/reports/199961/7.aspx*

organizations are constantly looking for ways to become more productive and to do less with more. I have heard this across all types of organizations including education, healthcare and even retail. Budgets are being frozen or worse yet, they are being cut. Departments aren't allowed to get any more FTE's (full time equivalents) meaning no more employees. The usual answer to this is for people to take on more duties and responsibilities which can lead to overwhelm, stress and burnout. This proves that burnout isn't just in our heads. But that is the first place we need to start in order to heal it.

We need to realize that burnout is something we need to pay attention to. Research clearly shows that mental stress of this nature creates inflammation in the body, which is one of the leading causes of heart disease, stroke, plaque formation, and increased susceptibility to cancer, autoimmune disorders, migraine, allergies and more.[2]

The main reason for feeling burned out is a loss for the passion that once drove us.

Working hard for something we don't care about is called stress. Working hard for something we love is called passion.

While it may not always be possible to rekindle that passion, it is possible to handle the way you deal with stress. Responding to the busyness crisis cannot be about adding more hours, hustling harder or grinding through it. It must be about thinking in a new way. It has to be managing your thoughts so that they serve you and what you are trying to accomplish. So while this isn't a productivity book in the normal sense, it will help you become more productive.

---

[2] Niemark, N. (2018). *3 Simple Ways to Master Your Stress and Take Back Your Health*. http://www.neilmd.com/3-Simple-Ways-To-Master-Your-Stress.pdf

I came about this work because of struggles in my own life. As a business owner of a UPS Store, I found myself oftentimes running around putting out fires. I was never able to focus on the big picture; to work *on* the business instead of *in* the business. It was truly frustrating because I would go to a conference and get pumped up from all of the great ideas and think I'm going to go back and make a really big difference! However, I kept finding myself getting sucked back into the weeds by the very next weekend. What I finally realized was that it was because I was getting bounced around in emotional drama that many times I had brought upon myself.

I felt at the time that this was only pervasive in small business with entrepreneurs. After all, most entrepreneurs create a business out of passion, not always to do something they love, but the passion to work for themselves. At first, because they are doing everything on a shoestring budget, this leads to them creating a job for themselves because they can't afford employees.

But a business can't be run by someone in a 'job'. A business of any size needs to be run by a leader. The main distinction between the two is in the way they think and how they act upon that thinking. Great leaders are very intentional with their actions which means they are intentional with their thinking. They don't bounce around from one emotional crisis to the next nor do they get sucked in to drama that is spinning into nothingness.

What I have found is that the problem is not just one of entrepreneurs. It is also a challenge for many organizations and large businesses. The reason is because we don't take the time that is required to develop ourselves and our leaders from the inside. This is called developing soft skills. Many people are familiar with soft skills such as learning to be an active listener and a good communicator, but we aren't taught how to manage our thoughts, our minds and our emotions.

Here is how most managers get promoted to their roles. They are good in their job so we promote them to manager or leader, supervisor or director: in a word 'boss'. This promotion has huge ramifications if not done correctly because in most cases the person is moving from someone who is in charge of a process; to a 'boss' who is in charge of people.

This is a big distinction => Process to People.

The problem comes from the lack of personal and people development of these bosses. We are great at teaching the hard skills and processes. Hard skills are easier to train. They can be things like creating a report, taking someone's blood pressure or sweeping a floor. For a nurse manager that may mean creating schedules and policies or running a clinical risk report. For a restaurant manager it may mean balancing the till, running a cost spreadsheet on inventory or purchasing supplies.

What's lacking is the education on soft skills. Soft skills such as emotional intelligence, listening and communication skills and connecting with others are hard to teach, so most organizations don't. They promote people and then let them flounder until they figure it out on their own. The good news: this can all be learned and it all is built on the foundation of learning how to manage our minds.

Think of training in soft skills a lot like we train for any other type of skill. Just as a doctor has to go to medical school to learn how to diagnose and a teacher must learn how to put together a lesson plan, managing your mind and training for soft skills works much the same way. Once you learn how to do it, practice will make it so much easier. Learning to manage your mind by learning about your core values and how you intentionally want to show up is education and training at its best.

These are the skills that stem from developing one's internal self. The place where influence truly comes from.

Your technical skills probably got you here. But in order to be effective, you need to develop and hone your soft skills. The skills that come from knowing yourself and managing your mind. If you believe this to be true, you are in good hands. If you are a bit skeptical, then hang tight with me. I think you will learn something and perhaps even enjoy the ride.

Chapter Two

You are a leader.

Good leadership is nice, great leadership is priceless.

Leadership is influence. Plain and simple. To be a leader, you need to have followers. But at the very root of having followers is making a connection with others.

As every other leadership guru out there has stated, it is not about titles, or seniority. It is not about office space, location, etc. It is about moving people in a direction.

In a word, Influence.

And guess what? Everyone has influence. Everyone. Think about it. Think about when someone walks into a room. Think about when your husband, your mom, your boss or your coworker walks into the room. Sometimes they brighten the room and add energy, and sometimes they don't. Sometimes they draw people to them like a sunbeam. Other times they detract the minute they darken the door. The key point is that every single person has energy and influence of some sort. Thus, we are all leaders.

With this premise, all you need to do is work on how you want others to feel and experience your leadership. When people connect with you, they will trust you. Once they trust you, they will follow you and more importantly, they will support you.

Trust of this nature comes from you acting congruent with what you say. In order to be in alignment like that, you need to really know yourself. This book is about finding and knowing yourself to be the most effective person, the most effective leader, you can be.

Before we get started let's look at the definition for effective.

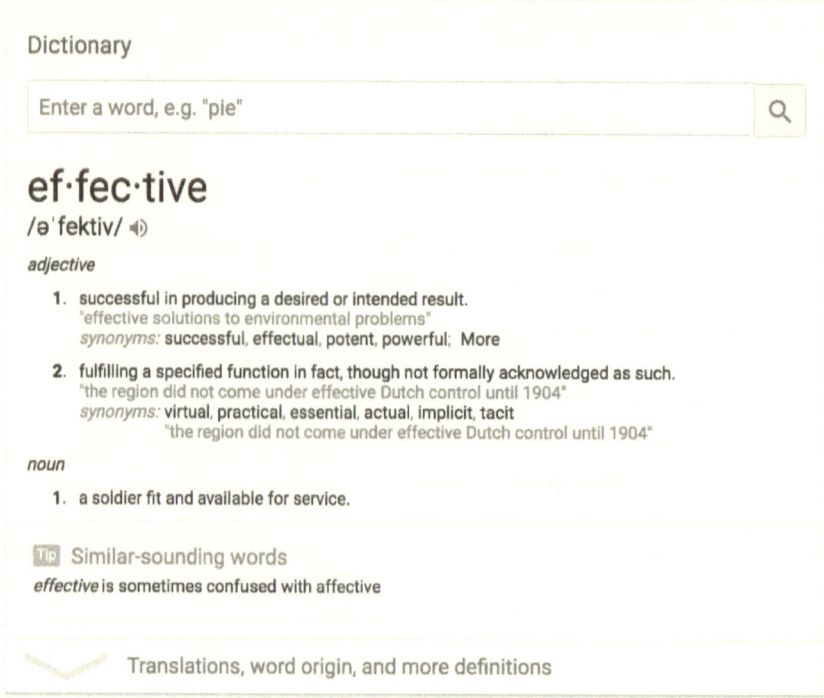

Effectiveness will give you back your life. It will help you create the balance you are striving for. Soon you will see that you have plenty of time. You will be productive. You will foster better teamwork and ownership in your team. And you will have time for the things you want to consume your day.

In order to be effective, you need to know what you want, be brave enough to stand in that truth and find where you are holding yourself back. This is what we will take on in the next chapters.

> **Key takeaway:**
>
> To be effective your actions need to be in line with your thoughts and values.

Chapter Three

Creating your life with intention.

Life is not about finding yourself, life is about creating yourself.

As a constant tinkerer, crafter and artist, I realized long ago that we can create the life we want.

Besides being a great quote in and of itself. It became much more than that for me. It became the basis for studying my life and living intentionally. Intentionality is the game changer. It is the catalyst. The 1°F that turns water into steam.

Basically, when you live in intention, great things happen. Do you want to know why? Because **thoughts become things. Literally.** In his groundbreaking book titled *The Biology of Belief*, Bruce Lipton actually proves from a biological standpoint how our thoughts not only have the power to change our well-being, but can also change our cell's makeup (i.e. our physical bodies) as well.[3]

So, let me ask you this, are you creating your life?

With purpose and intention?

Truly?

---

[3] Lipton, B. H. (2016). *The biology of belief: Unleashing the power of consciousness, matter & miracles*. Carlsbad, CA: Hay House.

Or are you letting an endless stream of circumstances, thoughts and beliefs carry you down a path that you haven't even chosen, like a flooding river? Are you letting other people's demands run your career and life?

As a recovering P3 (people pleasing perfectionist - make note of this as I will refer to it more than once), I found myself not once, not twice, not even three or more times doing what I thought *I SHOULD*. Over and over again, I was doing things because I wanted people to like me, love me and yes, approve of me.

And before you even ask, this definitely started in childhood. I mean I was the oldest of four girls after all. The whole world revolved around me ... until it didn't. Once sister number two came along, there was much perceived competition for my Dad's attention and love. I played trombone because he did. I showed cattle because he did. I got good grades, yada, yada, yada. You get the picture.

But this isn't about psychotherapy. We don't need to bring up, discern, or free-associate about my past. No, my friends, this is about now. This is about how I have learned and continue to learn how to live my life on purpose. Living life on purpose brings freedom and joy.

In his famous book, *How to Win Friends and Influence People*, Dale Carnegie wrote about Dr. John Dewey's study that "the deepest urge in human nature is the desire to be important."[4] Everyone wants to know their purpose. What they are put on this earth to do. How they fit into the bigger picture.

Knowing our purpose also helps us become more effective as leaders. In addition to my personal insight, I have gotten really good at studying people in leadership positions. As you have

---

[4] How to win friends and influence people. Dale Carnegie, Chapter 2.

probably noticed from your own experience, a position does not make a leader - let alone an effective one.

I have watched similar people with similar hard skills who have excelled in their jobs get promoted and lead in totally different ways. I have seen where one person seems to go about their day in relative ease, accomplishing many things without ever getting flustered while the other one is so 'busy' that they just seem to be whirling through life like the Tasmanian Devil.

Have you ever wondered why they are like that and how some of them get so much stuff done?

It is because they are being *intentional*. They are acting on *purpose*. They aren't consumed by what other people think. They don't live in constant emotional drama and turmoil, believing every self-defeating thought they have. You can't accomplish big things, the things you want to do with your life, if you are afraid to make a move.

This book will teach you how to keep P3 at bay and how each and every day you should question the thoughts that don't seem to serve you. When you combine this practice, with managing your energy and playing to your strengths, you will start rocking your life and work will be easier for you.

Not only will you start to begin to feel less stress, but leading and managing others will start to go smoother for you as well and you will begin to feel more at ease.

> **Key takeaway:**
>
> Are you being intentional with creating your life?

Chapter Four

Priorities aren't enough.

You make time for what you want. If you're not prioritizing the things you say you care about, consider the possibility that you don't actually care about those things.

~ **Elle Luna**

To accomplish our big goals and live the lives we want to create, we need to not only be productive human beings, but we need to be effective. To become effective, a.k.a. producing your desired result, requires being intentional. It requires you to chart a path and stay on it. Most leaders know this. It is the basic definition of success.

You may be thinking that to be more effective, you need to get your priorities straight. This is true.

So, let me ask you, why haven't you done it? Is it because you don't know what you need to do? Or is it because everything seems to be a priority?

I am guessing it is the latter.

I understand as it is the same in my world. For instance, as I sit here typing this I can think of a dozen things that need to move to the top of my list. Yet, a wise person once told me:

Everything is *important*. Not everything is a priority.

In a world that is constantly evolving, where the sand seems to literally shift under our feet, it is easy to get inundated and overrun by priorities.

Project #1 is a priority until your boss comes along wanting project #2 to be a priority. Not long after, a coworker piles on priorities #3, #4 and #5. Then you get a call from your patient, client, customer, or board member that adds on other priorities.

"People are feeling overwhelmed. Your patients are overwhelmed. Your staff is overwhelmed. Your leaders are overwhelmed" Joshua Freedman, CEO of Six Seconds.[5]

In today's crazy busy world, it is easy to be in constant reactionary mode. This state of constant overwhelm leads to disconnect. Disconnect from others who perceive your actions in the wrong way. Disconnect from family who wonder why you need to be working so much. And disconnect from your purpose.

All of this disconnection leads to feeling of overwhelm and more importantly, increasing levels of stress.

In small business, it takes owners a long time to realize that you need to be working ON your business as much as IN your business.

For leaders in any workplace scenario, the same is true. If you work in a big organization, your business is *you*. When is the last time you took an hour or two and worked on you? Without being told to or by just attending some trade conference? Do you ever take the time to contemplate how you can be more intentional and act on purpose?

As leaders, we are busy. That is not even in question here. But our busyness can derail us. It can keep us from putting some intention behind our actions.

---

[5] *https://www.6seconds.org/2018/03/21/healthcare-wellbeing/*

I know, I know…you can barely keep your head above water. But if you ever want to get to the surface and float on with ease, you need to take this seriously. It's even more important if you want to get ahead.

These are skills that can be learned. You can learn to notice where you have been in reactionary mode. To see where you hold yourself back. To notice when you don't speak up. Or worse yet, when you act like someone you don't even recognize.

Admit it, there have been times where you leave a conversation and think, "What the heck just happened?!? Why did I agree to that?" or worse yet, "Why did I say that?"

Sometimes our egos start to run the show. The P3 in us starts to take over thinking that we need to say yes in order for people to like us. But let me emphasize that in order to end the constant barrage of *busyness,* you need to become intentional. Intentional in thought and word and action.

Like a mechanic can diagnose engine problems, you too can diagnose where you lose your power. Once you figure out where your time and energy are going, you will be able to decide how you want to show up and what you want to do in the manner in which you want to do it. How awesome is that?

As a lifelong student on the subject of leadership, I have spent more than the required 10,000 hours to become an expert. Yet there are still times I am astounded at how I act. When we are under pressure our lizard brain kicks in.

The limbic system is in the oldest part of the brain and referred to as lizard brain because that is the only thing lizards have to work with. This part of our brain is responsible for thoughts of what I think of as the all-important F's: fight, flight, feeding, fear and fornication.

Back in cave-dwelling times, fight or flight was a response that was literally the deciding factor between living or dying. For the majority of the population today, this is no longer a necessary or correct response. However, situations that incite perceived fear can make us instantly feel the same response. It is automatic.

Picture this: you just walked out of a highly anxious, stressful conversation with your boss. The first thing you do is immediately head to your desk and wolf down an entire sleeve of Oreo cookies. Never mind the fact that you have given up sugar and flour and done so well all week.

All of the sudden, the guilt sets in. You start feeling shame and remorse. To make it worse, you start berating yourself for lack of willpower, thinking you are a loser and wondering what the heck just happened.

There are countless different versions just like this that we can experience each and every day. Perhaps your intention is to stop gossiping negatively about other people. But the situation presents itself and you just can't stop.

Or maybe you are the consummate people pleaser and someone asks you to take on one more project. You accept, even though you have been buried for weeks.

While maybe not fear-inducing scenarios in and of themselves, they all have a root of fear in them. You gossip because you want to fit in. You take on more work because you want others to like you. You eat because you get stressed and all of the sudden your body craves sugar and the Oreos seem to help calm you down in the moment.

Combine this with automatic responses that you have learned and hardwired over the years and you will soon realize that the lizard brain has been at work.

The lizard brain can definitely sabotage us. However, combine this with the ego and you have a propane leak just looking for a match. The ego is always trying to protect us from shame and failure. The lizard brain sees opportunities for shame and failure everywhere. Soon we are doing whatever it takes to just get by without dealing with the issue at hand or the feelings that come with it.

This is why priorities aren't enough. It is also why willpower alone won't work or at the very least won't sustain. So, see there is a reason you are swamped by busyness and seem to get stuck. You were just attacking it in the wrong way. Once you decide to make a study of your life and who you are, you will find ways to train your brain so that you can totally blow your own mind and your productivity out of the water.

> **Key takeaway:**
>
> New thinking will create bigger and better results.

Chapter Five

Why should anyone want to be led by you?

Leadership is not about titles or positions or flowcharts. It is about one life influencing another.

~ John Maxwell

Since we have now established that you are indeed a leader and that to become effective means so much more than reorganizing your priorities, we will take the time to set the foundation for how you want your influence to be felt and experienced.

Here is *the* thing:

Leadership is influence. But before leading others, we need to be able to lead ourselves.

Have you ever found your child saying something that you did? Or heard yourself say something your mom always said?

Human beings are social animals. We take our cues from those around us and most of the time those cues aren't verbal.

There is an often-used quote that states that only 7% of communication comes from the words we use and the rest comes from our body language and voice inflection. This suggests that what we are putting out into the universe; our energy and our actions, needs to be congruent with what we are saying.

The way we act is amplified when we are a leader. If your team sees you flipping out over the smallest things, creating emotional drama where it isn't needed, or making everything about you, they will act in kind which will just add to any type of emotional breakdown you are headed for.

To determine how you want your influence to be felt, you need to get clear on how you want to show up.

You need to decide this ahead of time, ahead of any situation in which you may get into an emotional windstorm, feeling overwhelmed and at your breaking point. Otherwise, you will fall into default mode which means you will start reacting to everything that comes your way rather than being proactive. Proactivity requires intentionality.

True intentionality requires us to stay a course according to how we want to show up, to act and react on purpose.

To become clear about what you want and why you want it begins with you. Clarity starts with knowing yourself.

I recently came across this question in an article[6] from Harvard Business Review.

Why should anyone (want to) be led by you?

What is your answer? Before we move on, take some time think about it. Try to answer it truthfully before you read on.

This is an ingenious question. Here's why.

Knowing yourself and growing yourself help you gain mental and emotional clarity. - John Maxwell

---

[6] Jones, R. G., Goffee, R., & Jones, G. (2015, November 23). Why Should Anyone Be Led by You? Retrieved from *https://hbr.org/2000/09/why-should-anyone-be-led-by-you*

John lives, breathes, writes and speaks about leadership. In his book, *Everyone Communicates, Few Connect*, John describes the importance of knowing yourself to be a great leader. He surmises this idea by saying, "You know what you do and don't know, what you can and cannot do. You are comfortable in your own skin and identity."

Clarity comes from getting to know yourself and getting comfortable with who you are. This takes understanding yourself.

Before we get to know you, let me ask you a question to help. How do you learn to know someone else?

You ask them questions. Questions about what they do for work and for hobbies. About what past times they enjoy. Questions about what makes them laugh, and what makes them cry.

My husband and I have this silly game we play in the car. When a conversation has hit a lull or become stagnant, especially on those long drives, I will say, "Tell me your hopes, your dreams, your desires." He and my son have gotten to a point where they get past rolling their eyes and know it's time to start asking questions.

Sometimes the question is simple, like "What is your favorite color and why?" Sometimes it is more about our dreams such as "If you could go anywhere in the world, where would it be?" No matter what the questions are, they always lead to richer, deeper conversation. We talk about where we want to travel and things we'd like to see, people we would like to meet, and so much more. Part of the magic of our game is that we are each other's captive audience. There is nowhere else to go and it is easy to turn off the music.

This is the same tactic you need to take with yourself. For your exercise, find an enjoyable place to sit. Get your favorite beverage and some music if you so desire. Journaling of this nature will become a habit if you do it in place that you find enjoyable. It will also become more fulfilling if you can find a time where you won't be interrupted. For many, that place is in solitude. Where they can get quiet enough to hear themselves think. But for others, that place may be a coffee shop, a park, or sitting in the city with a window open. The place doesn't matter as much as the stuff that comes out of you.

Don't be tempted to skip this process. For some reason, getting stuff out of your head and onto paper has magical properties. It is the quickest way to get to know yourself, your dreams, your desires, and what makes you tick. If you are easily distracted, try searching for air conditioner noise on YouTube. The hum in the background has a truly soothing effect.

In the paragraphs that follow, there are some prompts to get you going. If you would prefer to work on paper, you can download the workbook at *www.kathybourque.com/busyness-workbook*.

For every question, expound on the issue by imagining that I am there, right by your side, whispering in your ear *"and why?"*.

There is a tool used when trying to get to the root cause of something. It is called the 5 Whys. It is to ask why until you get to the very bottom of the issue or problem. You can use this to get to the bottom of your true happiness.

Take for example my love of travel. When I use the 5 Whys, while thinking about why I love to travel, I get to this: my love of travel is really a thirst for knowledge. It looks like this: I absolutely love to travel. Why? I like to see new places. (Key word: new, not old or going to the same place over and over). Why? I like to explore and find things out. Why? I have this want to know more, i.e. A thirst for knowledge.

Now it's your turn.

What is your absolute favorite way to spend your free time? (And why?)

If you have traveled, where was your favorite place you went and why?

Where do you still want to go?

Why do you want to go there?

What is it you like about traveling?

What don't you like about traveling?

Who is your favorite person from your past?

Who is your favorite person from your present?

Who would you like to meet?

What is the common theme among these people that you admire?

What drives you crazy about your significant other?

> Your family?

> Your coworkers?

Do you ever see that same quality in yourself?

What is one trait that you possess that you would like to make bigger or better?

What have you liked best about your job?

What do like the least?

What are the three things that bring you the most joy?

What could you do for hours on end without getting paid and for no other reason than the fact that you love to do it?

Why do you like doing that so much?

What can you be grateful for today?

As you are beginning to see, becoming an effective leader is more than setting priorities and being productive requires so much more than a to-do list. The most effective leaders know themselves really well and take time for reflection to learn more. This time is called whitespace.

The core of it all is your mind. Managing your mind requires awareness and practice. This practice is one that you need to incorporate into your life on a regular basis because what I have found is that creating whitespace is the practice that sets the great leaders apart.

> **Key takeaway:**
>
> To connect with yourself and others - be inquisitive. Always ask questions.

Chapter Six

The battle cry for whitespace.

Taking time to do nothing, often brings everything into perspective.

~ Doe Zantamata

The previous chapter may have been something new for you or it may have been something you already practice. If not, you may be feeling a little uncomfortable. So, let me ask you, do you ever just sit and enjoy some downtime? Without folding the laundry or playing candy crush? What about in the morning with your coffee or tea? How about then? Can you sit for 10-15 minutes without doing anything at all? No Instagram, Facebook or looking at your phone. Can you do it?

I tell you that there are times I struggle with it. Perhaps it's because I have worked more than one job for most of my adult life. Or maybe it's the fact that I feel there is still so much for me to learn and do. Perhaps, it's just plain old-fashioned guilt.

Early on in my own leadership journey, my mentor asked what our definition of a good weekend was. I said I really enjoy when I can fall into bed at the end of the weekend and think of the long list of things I accomplished.

He thought for a moment and then said "What would happen if you couldn't do that?"

I didn't answer. The minutes ticked by, creating an awkward heavy silence.

I mean I don't have a problem relaxing. Do I?

There are many times I love to sit out on my deck and enjoy the view after-all. But it's usually after I have mowed the lawn, worked the flower beds, finished the laundry and gotten everything ready for the week.

But if I couldn't do all of that, would I be able to just sit around?

On vacation – absolutely. At my sister's house in Illinois – no problem. But at home??? Was he nuts?

However, since then, I have learned the power of meditation and walking and yoga. The power of giving my mind time to decompress and breathe for a bit. Heck, sometimes I even take a nap. Gasp!

Dr. Henry Cloud refers to this as White Space.[7] Creating downtime or whitespace is essential to creating intention. The brain is under constant bombardment from our always-on, hyper-connected lifestyles. When we push our brains for too much and for too long, they can stall. Therefore, we need to create pockets of whitespace where we let them rest.

This is becoming more well-known as neurologists study the brain. Numerous case-studies prove that when we don't give our brains this much needed rest, they can stall. Dr. Cloud compares it to a computer that crashes because it is using too much memory. I'm sure that you have probably experienced this at the end of a busy

---

[7] Cloud, H., PHD. (2018, June 08). Why We Need WhiteSpace. Retrieved from *https://globalleadership.org/articles/leading-yourself/why-we-need-whitespace-dr-henry-cloud/*

day when you can't seem to decide what to have for dinner. This is called decision fatigue.

Not only have they found that decision fatigue is real, they have also found that our brains create neural pathways or information superhighways. Our brains our meant to become efficient. Once they learn something, it's stored in a place that is easy to find for the next time a similar event or task happens. This is why willpower can fail.

Have you ever gone home after work and binged on junk food after a day of doing so good? It can truly be from decision fatigue. If you have been making small decisions all day long, when it's time to pick a healthy choice over that cookie, your brain may be too tired to think – literally! When it is too tired to think a new thought, it will always choose an old familiar habit. Think of it as deciding to take a small dirt road versus a familiar interstate you have driven every day for the past 20 years on your commute. It will always choose the latter.

So, do your brain and your diet a favor, and incorporate some downtime into your routine. It will give you the clarity you need to prioritize. If it helps, quit calling it or thinking of it as downtime. Start thinking of it as your supercharger to success.

Practice it now. Take 5 minutes to sit and focus on your breathing.

> There are a couple of different exercises you can try. One I like goes like this:
>
>> Step 1: inhale in a nice slow breath and focus on the word *yes*.
>>
>> Step 2: exhale slowly while focusing on the phrase *thank-you*.

Your mind will wander. That is okay. When you notice this, don't beat yourself up, just refocus on the words and breathing. There is another exercise called the 4-7-8 technique by Dr. Weil. Here is how to use this technique:[8]

> Step 1: inhale for a count of 4
>
> Step 2: hold your breath for a count of 7
>
> Step 3: exhale for a count of 8

One word of caution: this technique is actually used to help people go to sleep, so only do it for three or 4 cycles.

After you get relaxed, ask yourself these questions (if you prefer not to write in your book, or are on a kindle, you can download the exclusive workbook at (*www.kathybourque.com/busyness-workbook*):

What are my top 3 priorities right now?

What is stopping me from getting these done?

Do I have the resources necessary?

What do I truly need to get my goals done?

Are the challenges I see just excuses?

Remember that the reasons you aren't accomplishing your goals are just excuses. If you keep making the same excuse for something over and over then it isn't a priority. When you see this with clarity, you will realize that you have two options. You can either figure out how to make it a priority or else dump it all together.

Can you let go of reasons and excuses? If you can, it will lead to insight.

---

[8] Weil, A. M.D. (2018) *https://www.drweil.com/health-wellness/body-mind-spirit/stress-anxiety/breathing-three-exercises/*

You may also want to ask yourself: How am I currently spending my time?

Find ways to be honest with yourself. It sometimes helps to do a weeklong time audit of yourself. Log everything you do into a calendar. At the end of the week, see where your time is going.

Do you find yourself in too many hallway meetings to mention? What is the first thing you do in the morning? Do you automatically check Facebook or email?

Now that you know your priorities and where your time is going, you might think you could stop reading this book. In fact, many mediocre leaders do just that. I am sure you can think of several in your own life who are great at setting their priorities yet still never seem to get anything done.

However, if becoming an effective leader was just about setting priorities, I am guessing you would already be one. Just because you set priorities doesn't mean that you will stop running getting pulled into emotional drama. So, take this down time to get real with yourself, to be authentic. This is the only true path to becoming an effective intentional leader.

> **Key takeaway:**
>
> Whitespace is a supercharger. Where can you incorporate it into your day?

Chapter Seven

The simplicity of one thought.

Is it true?

~ Byron Katie

That question was the true catalyst in my journey.

Up until that point, I had taken several leadership development classes. Classes on managing change. Classes on becoming more productive. Classes on learning about networking, first impressions and negotiation. However, none of those could prepare me for what I learned by asking the question: Is it true?

You see, before that question, I knew that I was *right*. I stood strong and proud in my beliefs and convictions. I knew that the way I saw the world was *the way* - the right way.

When I argued with others, including my spouse and family, I never backed down. Why, you might ask? Because I was right.

When I made a judgment about people, I knew I was *right*. When I found myself saying, "Who doesn't know that????" incredulously, I thought I was *right*.

That was until I met Byron Katie. I say met as if I truly met her in person. What I mean, of course, is that is when I found her book. It had such a huge impact on my life that I wish I could meet her and thank her in person.

It was around 12 years ago. At the time, my great aunt Betty (we'll call her GAB) lived north of Des Moines. I adored GAB. She was the practical jokester of the family. People just enjoyed being around her. My son was around 2 at the time and he loved being around her. *I* loved being around her.

Des Moines is smack dab between where I live and where my mom lives. It took us each about seven hours by car to get there. I often told Mom that she should call me when she was planning on going to visit GAB as I would love to visit and spend time with all of them.

My mom and I are close, but only call each other once every couple of weeks or so. Sometimes depending on how busy we are, it can creep into three or four weeks due to phone tag. This must have been one of those times because for some reason I had no idea that she and Aunt Faye (her twin) had gone to see GAB the weekend before.

I was outraged! How could she not call me? Did she not want to see me? What about her grandson? We live so far away after all. It's not like we get together all the time. I couldn't figure out why this was happening to me.

I was hurt as well. My thoughts made the circumstances mean so much. The conclusion I was jumping to was not good.

She didn't love us. How could she? A loving mother would have called. A loving mother would want to see her oldest daughter. A loving grandmother would want to see her grandson every chance she got.

My indignation was true and I knew I was *right*.

What I found out later is that it was a spur of the moment trip. She didn't want to call me because she didn't want me to feel guilty knowing I couldn't change my schedule that quickly. The fact of the matter was that she had many good reasons for not calling me. But my mind didn't even begin to think of any of those. It didn't even consider going to the place of thinking that she might have been doing it for MY own good.

Fast forward to just a few weeks ago. My husband and I were having a conversation about downsizing. As part of our grand plan to buy an RV and work remotely someday, I have decided that I need to start clearing things out of our massive, oversized house. In my effort to do this, I came across Marie Kondo's book, *The Life Changing Magic of Tidying Up*. It truly is a game changer if you are wanting to declutter your home.

In my excitement of clearing out years' worth of crap, clothes I hadn't worn, shoes that killed my feet and 5000 unmatched socks, I shared with my husband how he should try doing some of this truly liberating elixir of an exercise.

To say it didn't go over well would be an understatement. The main reason is because he has a lot going on right now and didn't want to add one more thing to his pile of things to do. However, my mind took it as he was reneging on our deal. It wasn't until I was telling my sister about the conversation that I questioned my thoughts and perceptions.

I said, "I don't know what I'm going to do because now he doesn't want to downsize and get the RV and there goes our semi-retirement plans!"

She asked, "What exactly did he say?"

"Well he said he doesn't want to downsize right now."

"Okay, did you hear the part about 'right now'? Perhaps he is just overwhelmed with all you have going on at the moment and the thought of trying to go through stuff just sounds excruciating. Do you know for a fact that he is thinking that? Is it true????"

Wow she was good! Can you see what would have happened if I had reacted to this like so many other times before? Honestly, these are the types of situations that cause break-ups, divorce and family feuds. Sometimes, when we are in the middle of something that is a high-stake issue for us, where emotions get kicked into a firestorm, it is hard for us to pull ourselves out and see a situation for what is truly happening. This is when the question, "Is it true?" can help us pause and get back to neutral.

Getting to neutral is essential for leaders. Have you ever experienced a manager that flips out from the smallest issues? It usually doesn't go well.

Take my co-worker Michelle. Michelle was like this. She struggled with insecurity. She often made mountains out of molehills because she took things personally and went right into reactionary mode. The immense pressure she felt to always be 'on', left her feeling drained an unable to make sound decisions. She came to me when she felt she was at her wits end and about to be fired. The first trick I taught her to help her get her emotions in check and get back to neutral was the "to-me edit".

When your mind starts to spiral out of control in a situation like this, omit the 'to me'. Undoubtedly, there is always a 'to me'. Just like I learned in the situation with my mom. My thoughts were "Why is this happening to me?"

When you find yourself saying this it means that you are personalizing the situation. Circumstances are always neutral. The meaning that you attach to them are what cause suffering. Next time you find yourself in a situation like this where you are thinking similar thoughts, take off the 'to me'.

Instead, ask yourself, "Why is this happening?"

Look for *unobjective facts* - not thoughts and try to get to the root of what is going on.

Where are the emotional storms in your life when your thoughts get hijacked into creating a reality where you know you are *right*?

Maybe you are like a former client of mine, Missy. She kept having struggles with coworkers. She liked to call them all 'Sally'. They frustrated her to no end. They were hard to get along with and never let her get her work done. Because of them, she kept trying different positions. She switched jobs, companies and even industries. But no matter where she went, there was a Sally.

Finally, she figured out that maybe the problem wasn't with Sally. The way she figured this out what by asking herself the question, "Is it true?"

Which prompted her to ask herself more questions, like "Could it be possible that the problem is with me?"

She found out that it was with her. Or more importantly her mind.

She was letting her thoughts run rampant and following them like a dog chasing its tail. Round and round, never getting anywhere but frustrated. It truly was a vicious circle.

Until one day it wasn't.

One day she learned to question her thoughts. To move from being stuck, to moving forward.

What worked for me and Missy can work for you too. These exercises are game-changers. So, try them and use them often. The next time you find yourself in the middle of an emotional thunderstorm, question what you know to be true. This is the first part to deconstructing the thoughts that no longer serve you. Next, we are going to work on what you *want to think* instead.

> **Key takeaway:**
>
> All you have to remember to ask: Is it true?

Chapter Eight

Values - Let your soul speak

Let the world know you as you are, not as you think you should be, because sooner or later, if you are posing, you will forget the pose, and then, where are you?

~ **Fanny Brice**

Choosing our thoughts with intention and deciding how we want to show up in the world depends on knowing what we truly value.

As mentioned earlier, we all have influence. Just by walking into the room there is an energy about you, an aura that follows you wherever you go just like the blanket that Linus carries in those Peanuts cartoons. (Hopefully yours isn't smelly and cloudy.)

Influence depends on wholeheartedness. Finding your values and living by them is at the center of being wholehearted. Leadership gurus Kouzes and Posner state in the *Leadership Challenge* that "Leadership is an affair of the heart."

There are many reasons that leadership is a heart matter. The first reason is because inspiration comes from the heart. As Kouzes and Posner write in their book, "you can't command people to commit, you must inspire them."

The second reason is that leadership thrives in an environment of connection. However, oftentimes, our ego (i.e. Our mind and all of its numerous thoughts) gets in the way. When this happens, it is necessary to be in a place where we can see the thoughts and voices in our head that undermine us. When we are in fear of being judged, we can act in ways that are not congruent with who we are.

In order to connect with others and lead from the heart, we need to be able to hear our heart and keep the voices of our mind at bay. Therefore, we need to be intentional about how we want our influence to be felt. The quicker you realize this the more you will work on yourself. This self-discipline of becoming aware and developing yourself is what is necessary in any leadership position. But here is the thing about influence, while it helps to be intentional with our influence by deciding how we want to show up, we need to do it from a wholehearted stance.

Brené Brown made vulnerability and wholeheartedness famous. In the *Gifts of Imperfection*, she wrote that in order to be authentic, you need to embrace your true self.

For many of us, we think we are showing up wholeheartedly and authentic - true to ourselves and our purpose. But if we have never really taken the time to question ourselves and what we want, our motives may not be as altruistic to ourselves as we think they are.

One day something may happen that makes us question it all. All of the sudden we feel tired of floating along doing what we thought we should be doing. For some, this is called a mid-life crisis. For others, it is an awakening. For Brown, it was what she termed the unraveling.

"The unraveling is a time when you are challenged by the universe to let go of who you think you are supposed to be and to embrace who you are."

For me, the unraveling was this persistent little whisper in my soul that kept telling me I was meant for more. More than being a college dropout who owned and operated a UPS Store. More than a small-town Midwestern girl who longed to help others. More than a leadership want-a-be. However, the P3 kept me playing it safe.

That was until a wise person told me that I needed to stop hiding and pretending, to show up and to be who I was.

He told me to show up and be me.

You see, I had been holding myself back.

This became apparent when I was asked to run for a position on the board of directors for our regional hospital. I'm not sure if you are aware of this or not, but hospital boards are made up of some pretty educated people. We are talking lawyers, accountants, the mayor; and those are just some of the laypeople (business people if you will). Then you throw in some doctors, nurses, etc. You get the picture. Here I was, little ol' small business owner who never finished college.

However, as my lifelong mantra has been to step outside of my comfort zone, I felt I had to do it. Even though there were more of us running than there were spots to fill. Even though my brain kept saying things like,

"What if I don't get it?"

"Who did I think am to sit on a board of directors of that caliber?"

I went ahead and ran. I got on and that is when I was sure they would all find out that I was a fraud. I had imposter syndrome and I had it bad. Imposter syndrome is where you doubt all that you have accomplished, chalking it up to luck and a bit of work. In addition to this, you are plagued with feelings that you don't belong and that people will find out that you are a fraud.

You see, they asked for my bio to publish in the paper. I still have a copy to this day. I tried to maneuver my way around the whole education thing. I mentioned my experience, my time in business, my family, and it worked!

At first, I was ecstatic, but soon, the imposter came roaring back in. What if they asked me questions I didn't understand? What if I was truly stupid? What if I said something awful and totally stuck my foot in my mouth?

Well many of those things did happen, except for the stupid part. While there are times when I still feel stupid, I have learned that the saying is true. *There are no stupid questions.* Because every time I have asked what appeared to be one, someone else chimes in to say, 'I'm glad you asked that. I was wondering that as well".

However, I wasn't always this enlightened.

At the time, I was taking my third leadership development class which felt a whole lot like therapy. I will never forget the day that my mentor called BS (as in bullshit) on my story. It was an intense master class with him and a few other students. Because of this, we had some true one on one time which provided ample space for many questions and reflection.

As an educator, he was the master of asking the tough questions. He was also very good at deciphering when someone was evading those tough questions.

We were talking about the board of directors and whatever the subject was, he could tell it was bothering me. While I don't remember the topic, I do remember that I hadn't spoken up to give my opinion. He asked me why I was staying quiet. I started hemming and hawing about the fact that I wasn't the educated one in these matters and that the 'experts' would know more about it.

That was when he literally threw his hand in my face and waved the big white BS flag. (At least that is how I remember it. It may have just been a simple question about why, but for now, we will stick with the drama of the big white flag.)

He said, "There is a reason you were asked to be on that board. There is a reason you are sitting at the table. You need to quit holding yourself back."

And then he said these words that would forever change my life.

He said, "You just need to decide how you want to show up and do it. Be it. Live it."

For my greatest power, my greatest leverage my greatest effectiveness, lies in being me. In being authentic to who I am at my core. Understanding this and more importantly, buying into this, is a huge step. But I warn you, if you agree to go down this path, it is just the beginning. For once you start, it instantly leads to another question which is:

"Who am I at my core?"

I had spent so much time trying to be liked by everyone, doing what I thought I was supposed to do, playing by the rules, that I wasn't sure what I really wanted, let alone knowing who I was.

Does this sound familiar? Perhaps you are thinking, you want your life to be different, in some way. You may be feeling stuck. Stuck in a job or position or business that no longer seems to fit.

Or worse yet, you may be feeling overwhelmed and exhausted. Tired of keeping up the charade - the false image of who you are and how you live your life. Believe me, it's easy to do.

> *It's never too late to be what you might have been.*
>
> **~ George Eliot**

Consider my client Becky. Becky owns and operates her own fitness business. She teaches healthy eating and exercise. Yet she is exhausted and feels like a total fraud. She gets so worn out that at night she binges on sugary 'health' foods full of empty calories. The next morning, she feels such shame that she forces herself to work out double or triple the amount she would teach any of her hardcore students to do. This in turn continues to fuel the cycle of exhaustion leaving her no time for her husband and kids. She is not even sure she wants to work out any more let alone teach others how to.

Or think about Abbie. Abbie has always been an overachiever. She got straight A's all through school, went on to get married, had 2 kids and a dog and has rapidly been working her way to the top of a large regional healthcare system. She's gotten everything she has ever wanted yet something still seems to be missing. She lately has been wondering if this is all there is. She's even starting to think that she was happier when she was a nurse making half the money.

Does any of this feel familiar?

Have you been on course your entire life, doing what you should, accomplishing great things but somehow, you feel that something is missing? Are you no longer sure of where you are going?

Have you placed your ladder against a wall, working your way up and recently found yourself wondering:

Is this all there is?

Do I want to climb up another rung?

Do I even have my ladder against the right wall?

You may be contemplating a new career. You might be feeling adrift in your relationships. Maybe you have started to hear the whisper of what you *want* to be doing. Scratch that, doing what you know you are meant to do deep down in your soul, vs. what you feel you *should* be doing.

Perhaps you are feeling overwhelmed. Scattered. Burning the candle at both ends. Taking care of everyone but yourself.

All of these are legitimate feelings. Many people, at one point or another, feel the desperate, clawing need to find their purpose. To find balance. At the very least to lead a life more in tune with who they really are and want to be.

I know I did. It's what led me here, writing this book for you. I am right here with you. Because I have been there and continue to be there at times. Feeling just as you are.

At the time, I appeared successful. I owned and operated a franchise, was a leader in my community, had a child, a dog and a great marriage.

But I knew I was destined for more.

I came to the conclusion that doing what I thought I was supposed to, what I should, wasn't enough. I needed to find my path, to create my journey.

My plan had just run out and it was time for a new one.

Whatever your case may be, I want you to keep this one question from Dr. Phil in mind as you go through the workbook,

"How's that working for you?"

All of the things I have put before you culminate into this one beginning seed. In order to be more effective, you need to set good priorities. Priorities that come from the clarity of knowing who you are and where you want to go. Priorities that are in line with the person you hear calling to you from the depths of your soul.

More than that, in order to connect with others and influence them - they need to know who you are, to trust you. This comes from being in alignment with your core values.

So, who are you? Have you sat with yourself long enough to answer that question, truly answer it?

It's important to know this inner part of you. To understand what you value.

It's not hard to make decisions when you know what your values are.

~ Walt Disney

The #1 reason to get real with yourself and to know your values is to be able to make decisions with clarity and ease.

Most people know what they value. Or think they do.

When going through my workshops, values can take a week or two to define.

You might be asking why. It is because values are so important to who you are. Think of a time when you agreed to do some 'thing' but soon after, started sabotaging that very same 'thing'. Or perhaps there was a time when something just totally felt wrong in your gut. These were probably times when your actions were not in line with your core values.

We get so wrapped up in climbing the corporate ladder, checking things off our list, moving the direction we were taught (graduate, get married, have 2.5 kids, get nice house, car, etc.) that we may not even realize that we never wanted all those things any way.

I see this all the time with business owners. They start their biz, they grow it some, then they need an employee to help keep up with demands, which prompts more growth and more employees, a bigger space, better website, etc. etc. etc.

STOP

Take a moment to breathe.

Who says that you have to grow your business exponentially?

Who said that in order to be happy you need 2.5 kids?

You may be thinking...

Who wrote these rules? & why am I following them?

This is good.

When you do this exercise, listen to your soul. Listen to that part deep down inside of you that whispers your true desires.

By taking time to do values work, you can start to make decisions in a new easier way. In a way that is in collaboration with your soul. Many times, we get into business or a career where we have to think a lot and make decisions. It can start to feel forced. Like we are grinding our way through them. You start to feel stress that keeps mounting until soon you want to scream because the answer just isn't coming to you. You feel like if you could just push a little harder or hustle just a teeny bit more, things will get better.

However, when you work in collaboration with your soul, you can listen for the answer. No more grinding through. Instead, sit with yourself. Ask yourself questions. Questions like,

"If I did know the answer, what would it be?"

"If future me was asked how I handled this, what would she say?"

Then listen without doubt or judgment. Many times, we know the answer but are too afraid to even think of it.

Our ego will start to throw up red flags in order to protect us. Usually it will sound like this,

"What will people think?"

"I'm not ready."

"Who am I to do that?"

"What am I thinking?"

To find and create your purpose, you need to write your own rules. Starting with what you value. By realizing your true values, you can start bringing more intention to your life. You can work from a place of being proactive instead of reactive which will bring a profound sense of meaning and purpose to your life, something we all crave. Much of the unraveling we experience comes from our loss of direction and purpose. We all want to feel that we are part of something bigger than ourselves. We want to know our purpose for existence. Values help to figure this out. They can guide you in many different ways.

First, values act like a beacon of light, showing us our path. They help us craft decisions that are in line with who we want to be and how we want to show up. They are absolutely necessary for living intentionally. Second, values act as a filtering mechanism that guides decisions and thoughts about what should be let in and what should be kept out. And third, values act as a magnet drawing you back to where you are supposed to be.

Many times, people will list out core values of what they think they should have.

The order usually goes like this:

God, Family, Work, Love, Honesty.

Take Emily, who took one of my workshops and started just like that, as in that exact order. When I asked her to dig a little deeper she realized that she thrives on being busy at work and often stays late because of some big project. What does this say about her stated values? Well, that, she is either lying to herself or she is truly out of sync which she had been feeling lately and had manifested into nightly quarrels with her spouse.

Values are tricky to define because we tend to look through the *aspirational lens* - the lens of what we want, instead of the *operational* lens of what we do. The true magic happens when you combine the two.

To get started, we will look through the operational lens. The one that shows us who we are as if it hit us up the side of the head. If you don't understand what I'm talking about, read through these statements quickly, listening to yourself for the answers.

- o **Wearing white pants after Labor Day is okay.**
- o **Letting your kids eat Halloween candy for dinner is acceptable.**
- o **It is alright to say the Lord's name in vain if I am really upset.**
- o **Gay marriage should be legal everywhere.**
- o **Our current leadership is crazy.**
- o **The death penalty should never be revoked.**
- o **Marijuana should be legal everywhere.**

Answers to those thoughts may be so visceral that you don't even have to think about them, your values will tell you exactly where you stand. In other areas in our life that don't seem so black and white, our values aren't always so clear.

Here are a few points about values:

1. Unless you value killing people or something else that is highly illegal and unethical, your values do not make you a bad person. i.e. Having career as your number one value does not make you a bad person.

2. Your values may change in priority (and usually do) over time. In your 20s you may very well value a career as number 1, whereas in your 30s and 40s that may change to family.

3. Your values need to be what is truly important to you and unfortunately there is no cheat sheet here. Only **you** can determine what you value.

4. If your place of employment does not value the same things you do personally, there will eventually be discord.

5. It is good to define your core values and put them in writing.

6. You need to test your core values through daily decision making.

Individuality comes from your soul and not through your head.

~ Thomas Moore

So, start brainstorming here and list out **any** and **all** core values. To get you started, I have created a list that is listed in the resources section. You can also find the list here: *www.kathybourque.com/core-values* or you can download the full workbook here: *kathybourque.com/busyness-workbook*.

Go through the list and circle all of the words that resonate with you, the ones that trigger an emotional response.

Ability	Abundance	Acceptance
Accomplishment	Achievement	Acknowledgement
Adaptability	Adequacy	Adroitness
Adventure	Affection	Affluence
Alertness	Aliveness	Ambition
Amusement	Anticipation	Appreciation
Approachability	Artfulness	Articulacy
Assertiveness	Assurance	Attentiveness
Attractiveness	Audacity	Availability
Awareness	Awe	Balance
Beauty	Being-ness	Belongingness
Benevolence	Blissfulness	Boldness
Bravery	Brilliance	Briskness
Buoyancy	Calmness	Camaraderie
Candor	Capability	Care
Carefulness	Certainty	Challenge
Charity	Charm	Chastity
Cheerfulness	Clarity	Classy
Cleanliness	Cleverness	Closeness
Cognizance	Comfort	Commitment
Compassion	Competence	Complacency
Completion	Composure	Concentration
Confidence	Conformity	Congruency
Connection	Consciousness	Consistency

Contentment	Continuity	Contribution
Control	Conviction	Conviviality
Coolness	Cooperation	Copiousness
Cordiality	Correctness	Courage
Courtesy	Craftiness	Creativity
Credibility	Cunning	Curiosity
Daring	Decisiveness	Decorum
Deepness	Deference	Delicacy
Delight	Dependability	Depth
Desire	Determination	Devotion
Devoutness	Dexterity	Dignity
Diligence	Diplomacy	Direction
Directness	Discernment	Discretion
Discipline	Discovery	Discretion
Diversity	Dreaming	Drive
Duty	Dynamism	Eagerness
Economy	Ecstasy	Education
Effectiveness	Efficiency	Elation
Elegance	Empathy	Encouragement
Endurance	Energy	Enjoyment
Enlightenment	Entertainment	Enthusiasm
Exactness	Excellence	Excitement
Exhilaration	Expectancy	Expediency
Experience	Expertise	Exploration
Expressiveness	Extravagance	Extroversion
Exuberance	Evolution	Facilitating
Fairness	Faith	Fame
Fascination	Fashion	Fearlessness
Fidelity	Fineness	Finesse
Firmness	Fitness	Flexibility
Flow	Fluency	Fluidity
Focus	Fortitude	Frankness
Freedom	Friendliness	Frugality
Fun	Gallantry	Generosity

Gentility	Genuineness	Giving
Grace	Gratefulness	Gratitude
Gregariousness	Growth	Guidance
Happiness	Harmony	Health
Heart	Helpfulness	Heroism
Holiness	Honesty	Honor
Hopefulness	Hospitality	Humility
Humor	Hygiene	Imagination
Impact	Impartiality	Impeccability
Independence	Industry	Ingenuity
Inquisitiveness	Insightfulness	Inspiration
Instinctiveness	Integrity	Intelligence
Intensity	Intimacy	Intrepidness
Introversion	Intuition	Intuitiveness
Inventiveness	Joy	Judiciousness
Justice	Keenness	Kindness
Knowledgeableness	Lavishness	Leadership
Learning	Liberation	Liberty
Liveliness	Logic	Longevity
Love	Loyalty	Majesty
Mastery	Maturity	Meekness
Mellowness	Meticulousness	Mindfulness
Moderation	Modesty	Motivation
Mysteriousness	Neatness	Nerve
Obedience	Open-mindedness	Openness
Optimism	Opulence	Order
Organization	Originality	Outlandishness
Outrageousness	Passion	Peacefulness
Perceptiveness	Perfection	Perseverance
Persistence	Persuasiveness	Philanthropy
Piety	Playfulness	Pleasantness
Pleasure	Plentiful-ness	Poise
Polish	Popularity	Potency
Practicality	Pragmatism	Precision

Preeminence
Privacy
Professionalism
Punctuality
Quietness
Readiness
Recreation
Relaxation
Resolution
Respect
Reverence
Sacredness
Saintliness
Security
Self-realization
Sensuality
Sexuality
Significance
Simplicity
Smartness
Solidity
Speed
Spontaneity
Strength
Success
Supremacy
Supremacy
Tactfulness
Thankfulness
Thrift
Traditionalism
Trust
Understanding
Usefulness

Preparedness
Proactivity
Prosperity
Purity
Quickness
Reason
Refinement
Reliability
Resolve
Restfulness
Richness
Sacrifice
Sanguinity
Self-control
Self-reliance
Serenity
Sharing
Silence
Sincerity
Sophistication
Solitude
Spirit
Stability
Structure
Sufficiency
Surprise
Sympathy
Teamwork
Thoroughness
Tidiness
Tranquility
Trustworthiness
Uniqueness
Utility

Presence
Proficiency
Prudence
Qualification
Realism
Recognition
Reflection
Resilience
Resourcefulness
Restraint
Rigor
Sagacity
Satisfaction
Selflessness
Sensitivity
Service
Shrewdness
Silliness
Skillfulness
Solidarity
Soundness
Spirituality
Stillness
Substantiality
Support
Superbness
Synergy
Temperance
Thoughtfulness
Timeliness
Transcendence
Truth
Unity
Valor

Variety	Victory	Vigor
Virtue	Vision	Vitality
Vivacity	Warmth	Watchfulness
Wealth	Wholesomeness	Willfulness
Willingness	Winning	Wisdom
Wittiness	Wonder	Worthiness
Zeal	Zest	Zing

After you have done that, group like words together into 5 different areas. For example, integrity, trustworthiness and loyalty could be one group whereas growth, abundance and prosperity could be grouped in another set. Once you have done this, circle the best word of the group that feels right. In the end it may look something like this:

integrity	abundance	acceptance	cheerfulness	directness
honest	growth	loving	**happy**	**honest**
trustworthy	prosperity	grace	humor	
honor	**creativity**	timeliness	kindness	
leadership		**empathetic**	joy	
		love	friendliness	

In the next chapter you will start putting your defined values into practice in order to show up as only you can.

> **Key takeaway:**
>
> Let your core values guide you daily by keeping them visible.

Chapter Nine

Labels - What's in a name?

I am.
Two of the most powerful words in the English language, for what you put after them shapes your reality.

~ Unknown

In order to live by your values, you need to be able to identify when something happens where you don't.

One thing that keeps us from living a life based in our values is our labels. Take a minute to think about how you identify yourself. Perhaps you are a mother, a father, a daughter or a son. Maybe you are a teacher, a doctor, a fireman or a banker. You could also be a golfer, a musician, a runner or an artist. Add to that the fact that you are an extrovert, a thinker, an analytical or an expressive. Not only do we wear more than one label, often times they can be piled on in such a wonky way that one may not necessarily go well with another.

From our born identities to our hobbies, passions and past-times, we accumulate labels. Some of our labels serve us while others hinder us and hold us back. Some we have chosen and others have been given to us.

This reminds me of a study we learned about in psychology class lesson covering self-awareness and when self-concept starts to develop. There was a researcher who went to a classroom of kindergarten students and asked the question,

"Who in here is a singer?" and they all raised their hands. "We are all singers!"

A few short years later, as those same children were entering middle school, that same researcher went back to the same class of students and asked the same question.

"Who in here is a singer?"

This time only half of the class raised their hands. Only half now considered themselves to be singers. Why? What had changed? Did they no longer have the passion to sing? Not really. What the study revealed is that it is at this time in life when we start to develop our self-concept.

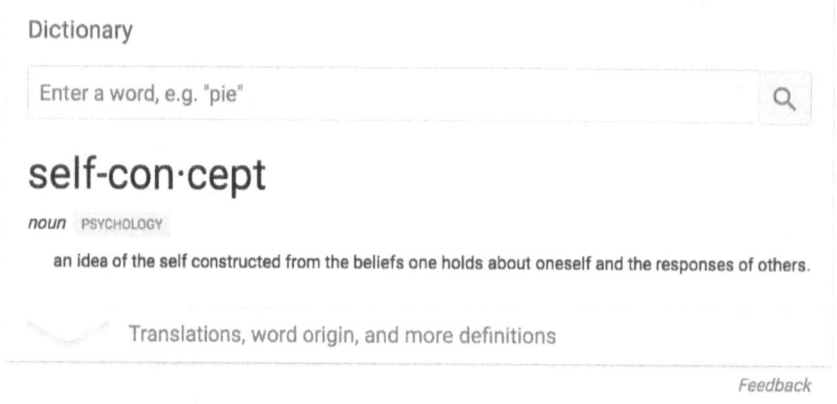

Remember, if you want to print a copy of this in a workbook format go to kathybourque.com/busyness-workbook.

Our self-concept holds a lot of power. With that in mind, think back to your early childhood to see when and where you have picked up some of your labels.

Now we will start to decipher some of yours.

What labels do you use to identify yourself? i.e. mother, husband, brother, wife, sister, daughter

List them all here:

What labels are you proud of?

What labels do you wish you didn't have?

Have you deliberately chosen all of them or are there some that were given to you?

What about the not-so-obvious labels we all give ourselves like boss, worker, volunteer, artist, etc.

Add those to your list.

Now I want you to think of your negative labels. Yes, we can have negative labels as well. Really, they are limiting beliefs that hold us back but for now we will think of them as something solid like a label. The reason for this exercise is to point out any excuses that you might have, any weaknesses or vulnerabilities.

For instance, one of my negative labels is that I am not a runner. For me, I sound like Darth Vader when I run. Which scares my brain because I am afraid I will hyperventilate, or suck the air right out of the person next to me. But the truth is, I don't like how I sound so I choose not to run.

In thinking about this label, it seems pretty absurd right? I mean most of us biped human beings can walk and if we can walk, we should be able to move our feet faster and actually run. Therefore, I can (literally) run and should think of myself as a runner.

However, I don't.

List your negative labels here.

Labels are important stuff.

They are the key to figuring out where we belong. Brené Brown explains it beautifully when she describes true belonging in her book *Braving the Wilderness*.[9] In her research on belonging, she found that people "want to be a part of something - to experience real connection with others - but not at the cost of their authenticity, freedom, or power."

Consider a friend of mine who announced that she is gay a few years ago. She is now openly talking with the family about being gay and how she wants to move to the coast. The conversation we had just a few weeks ago was about what type of lesbian she was.

As I was listening, I thought: What???? There are different types of lesbians???

I had no clue!

This led to further dissertation about what the characteristics and traits of each group were - in essence, she was trying to pick her label.

One of my other labels came from early in life. It is the 'good' label. You know the one I'm talking about. The one where you hear directly or indirectly how 'good' you are.

Things like, "Oh Kaye, you have such good girls."

Or 'be a good girl' - oh my gosh I've even used that with my son, "Be Good!"

I also heard things like "good job Kathy, you did everything right."

---

[9] Brown, B. (2016) Braving the wilderness: The quest for true belonging and the courage to stand alone. Farmington Hills, MI: Thorndike Press.

It isn't hard to learn that good equals; *well - good.* And everything else doesn't.

Soon I wanted nothing more than to be good. I wanted to be the smartest, the nicest, the easiest to get along with and yes, even the prettiest. I worked hard at being good. In my efforts, I was always trying to get everyone, and I do mean everyone, to like me. Which still haunts me to this day.

While this desire helps me learn the importance of seeing other people's perspectives, for which I am thankful, it also causes me to lose my own voice for fear of judgment. Then when I do use it, people seem surprised, saying, "wow, I've never seen this side of you". Which in turn makes me want to retreat and go back to being the 'good' girl.

But speaking your mind should never make you feel like you are being bad, insubordinate, evil, selfish or any other myriad of horrific terms that come to your mind. As long as you are not using the "brutal truth", speaking your mind, or better yet - your soul, is always the best option. Just remember there is a human being on the other side and always use grace and kindness.

I'm here to tell you that if your labels aren't aligned with where you want to go, you will find it much harder to get there, if not impossible. So, you need to be able to spot your labels and the thoughts behind them in order to start gaining traction to conquering your busyness.

Think about it.

With my 'I am not a runner' label, it would be very difficult for me to go out and run a 5K tomorrow. I might do okay for the first minute or so until I start the heavy breathing, about-to-hyperventilate, Darth-Vader thing. Quickly my brain will jump to the best way to stop any discomfort that I'm experiencing. And believe me, it doesn't hold back.

Oh no, quite the contrary. Soon it's pulling all the punches. Shouting at me "What are you doing? Who do you think you are? You are not a runner! You are going to kill us!!! Stop, for the love of Mary."

Until it moves on to the guilt - just like the church lady down the street who actually said tsk-tsk. "Fine, just know that if you break an ankle, you deserve it."

Then it will even move on to pleading. "Please stop. You. Are. SCARING ME!"

If you are saying to yourself, "oh I don't have those voices" think again. Right now, you are probably wondering about your Facebook feed, or what to cook for dinner...maybe there's a good recipe on Pinterest; squirrel!

Our minds our wired to run a constant narrative of what is happening to us. These are the semi-conscious thoughts we have. We also have thoughts that are more unconscious. They are the ones that drive things we have learned and hardwired such as walking and talking. For instance, reading this book: you are now moving your eyes across the page, interpreting their meaning, ignoring the hum of the refrigerator or the chirps of the cicadas outside, trying to stay focused.

There are different estimates to how many thoughts a person has per day, but the amounts are staggering. When thinking about the narrative thoughts alone, it could be in the tens of thousands. They are shaped by what we have learned, the culture we grew up in, the experiences we have had, the meaning we attach and the motives our egos have.

Just for fun, I tried to be aware and notice my mind chatter (that constant narrative) for a 3-minute span on my way to work one day. Here is what it said,

> *Wow the sun is beautiful this morning. Those cows remind me of 4-H, my Dad. Hmmm, I wonder if I should look for Tom Messer on Facebook. Probably won't do any good as I couldn't seem to find any of my old 5th grade Ashton friends. Which is now way younger than Cameron is. I can't believe he is going to be 15 this year. I wonder if he remembers that I told him we could do a birthday party with friends. He hasn't mentioned it yet. I won't remind him, with everything we have going on in our lives right now, Rick will never let him have that many kids over to spend the night. He needs to get up early and go fence. Probably needs to mow too. Did we remember to turn back on the sprinklers? That will muck up the windows. Note to self - call the window washers once I get to work. Boy, Sam sure was in a mood yesterday. I hope that isn't the case again today. He needs to go on vacation. Scotland, wow how I loved Isle of Skye. What was the name of that cute town? Hmmmm, Portsmouth, Port something I'm sure. Poretree? I will look that up as well. I can't wait to go back to Europe. Unfortunately, it won't be for a few years. That's okay because I was so lucky to get to go the first time. I love to travel.*

In the span of three minutes, my thoughts jumped between a wide array of many topics. This happens almost daily on my commute. Sometimes it takes me over 20 miles before my mind chatter stops to catch a breath and I notice that I have either tried to solve all of the world's problems, relived all of the past ones or am worried about the ones to come.

What I am trying to show you is that you are not your thoughts. Michael Senger talks about this in his book *The Untethered Soul*. When considering the soul, we need to realize that there was an I before I created the belief. Your thoughts can literally have a mind of their own and you can learn to see them for what they are: just ideas floating by trying to take hold. With practice, you can start to detect when your thoughts aren't serving you. Think of it like a surfer does a wave. They watch and wait for the perfect one to come in and then they ride it for dear life. You should do the same with your thoughts. Only pick the good ones. The ones that will serve you and where you want to go. This is a very important skill to learn.

We get so busy learning to play by all the rules we are given when we are brought into this life. So much so that we don't learn how to think for ourselves. We definitely don't learn that we don't have to believe all of the things we think. Take a moment to remember back in grade school where there was always a right answer. I LOVED those times. Where someone could give me the rules and as long as I followed them, I got As.

I was addicted to those rules. Even when there were times I chose not to follow them. At least I knew I was *choosing* to break the rules.

But here's the honest truth as I know it: there is no answer key to life. it is hard work that will never end. But it is also a lot of fun.

Hold the phone! Life doesn't come with that type of guidebook or set of rules? Yay! But wait one darn stinkin minute. How do I know what is right for me? Oh, I know. Go to college, get married, have a boy, then a girl, get an amazing job, have amazing kids, etc. Etc. Etc.

But what about when you miss a step, when you only have one kid, when you get a divorce, or hate your job, or do any number of things that make us feel like complete and utter failures.

What about then?

Good news for you my friend. That's what this book is about. The 'then' part. More importantly it's about having the training to know *what* to do for 'then'. Because if you have the right training, you can be prepared to take on any *'then'*.

First, we need to realize that the labels we use and the stories we tell ourselves are more precious real estate than the islands of Hawaii. We must learn to cultivate them and tend to them, much like a garden isle itself. We have to enrich the mind, nourish the field, nurture it with nutrients and get rid of the weeds. We must be vigilant about what we let in.

But oftentimes, by the time we figure this out, we have already taken on labels. Labels that create stories. Labels that define us and limit us. Stories that hold us back. This is why change and being intentional is so hard.

While it is hard, it is also doable. You just need to train your mind to start thinking in new ways. Now that you know how you identify yourself, we will continue to work on how you can get quicker at detecting your thoughts and beliefs.

> **Key takeaway:**
>
> What are you putting behind the all-powerful 'I am'?

Chapter Ten

Blinded by the Light - Becoming Aware

Argue for your limitations and sure enough they are yours.

~ Richard Bach

Now that you know what you value, how you see yourself and how you want to show up, you can start to identify where you are holding yourself back.

That's right, there are areas in your life where you are holding yourself back. Just as I was. There is no one that is doing it to you. There are no circumstances that make it so. It is you, your thoughts and your mindset. The good news is that it is totally fixable! All you have to do is start noticing when you say or do something that reinforces the limits you have put upon yourself.

You may think as your reading this that you never say these things, or have these thoughts. But that inner critic is a sneaky foe and can make fear look like the quest for more knowledge.

For instance, when do you think or say "I'm not ready."

When does the thought cross your mind that you'll just get one more certification and then you will be ready.

When do you hear a whisper that says "I can't do it now because now I'm not _____enough"?

Thoughts like these pop into our heads and we don't even question them. That is because fear doesn't fight fair. It will use old thoughts that are habitual and seem truly reasonable at the time. Your ego will try all types of these thoughts to keep you from making a complete and total fool of yourself. The key is that fear in this day and age is rarely deadly.

Remember the lizard brain? It is going to tell you to stop what you are attempting to do or to run for the hills, regardless of the size of the fear or how true it is.

Here is a perfect example. A couple of years ago, my bright, intelligent, sophisticated, highly-skilled-in-her-job sister Jill was looking at taking a new job offer in Indianapolis. There were so many reasons this was an amazing opportunity for her and her family that she could not pass up.

Her previous company wanted her to come back. They wanted her help to go and reshape a new market. She was the perfect candidate for it as she knew the company's culture and processes, plus had worked in the market for the competition. The move would get her back to the Midwest, in the same town as her in-laws and only hours from our family. Plus, it gave her the ability to grow her pay and benefits. All these things had her wanting the job just as much as the company wanted her. It was a perfect fit. Yet the imposter syndrome which pops up whenever the inner critic is at play, was still holding her back. In the month of conversations where we dissected the pros and cons, a couple of phrases kept coming out of her mouth.

The first was, "I don't know Kath, I don't think I'm ready."

"What? What do you mean you're not ready? What could possibly make you think that?"

"Well, remember the last time when I was the general manager of Champaign and things didn't work out quite right?"

"Well, they didn't necessarily work out wrong. You were young and brand new to management plus it was a tough market. Not to mention that was ten years ago. We all have to learn somewhere."

"Well, yeah, I guess…but what will people think?"

Huh??? "What do you mean when you say, 'what will people think?'"

"Well you know, we moved from Indy to Charlotte, to Michigan, Illinois, back to Charlotte…they will think I can't stick with anything."

"Or, just a thought here, they might think that you moved with the company all of those times to help in markets that needed you. I know I would think that you must have gotten a really good offer to move from Charlotte, knowing how much you guys love it there."

The rest of the conversation was more of the same. Her reasons for being asked were in most part because the CEO highly respected her and wanted her back on his team. He realized that she was the absolute best candidate for the job. But our minds forget things like that or simply try to diminish those things. For some reason, we humans like to latch on to our mistakes and our inadequacies. I am sure there is some psychological reason for that, but for now, we just need to learn how to notice it and deal with it because fear will throw up false reasons and excuses as to why we aren't ready for something all day long.

When we look at something the thing we look at changes.

~ Wayne Dyer

So, what does your thought or statement look like? Maybe it is something like, "What if I'm not the right fit?" or "What if this causes strife?" It may be the familiar, "I'm not sure." Or "I don't know."

Notice any time when you seem to be totally clouded concerning a decision and can't decide what to do. Times when you tell yourself, "I'm not sure". This is usually when our egos and minds are trying to protect us with that false fear. Key words to look for include just, once, maybe and yet. If you are having trouble seeing your signals of distress, ask a friend. Or think back to something you wish you would have done but made excuses as to why the timing wasn't right. Try to also notice places, times or circumstances when you don't speak up for fear of judgment.

Take writing this book, I started asking myself,

"Who am I to do this?"

"Am I qualified to write a book?"

What's worse, once I decided to write it, the closer I was getting to being done, the louder my fears got. My thoughts turned to, "Oh screw it. This was a stupid idea anyhow. No one will ever know that I was going to do this. What was I thinking!"

But then I remembered the following quote and thought that if someone like Maya Angelou struggled with this, then I am in amazing company.

I have written 11 books but each time I think 'Uh-oh, they're going to find out now. I've run a game on everybody, and they're going to find me out.'

~ Maya Angelou

It is estimated that nearly 70% of adults deal with imposter syndrome. In my research for my master's degree, I found that it literally can affect anyone, from bankers, teachers and librarians, to doctors, dentists and administrators.

The researchers, Dr. Pauline Clance and Dr. Suzanne Imes,[10] conducted over 150 interviews back in the '70s that led to naming this phenomenon. Since then numerous studies have been conducted pointing to the fact that it usually affects high achievers who feel lack of internal success and instead credit their journey to luck.

So, why does imposter syndrome specifically affect leaders and continually try to hold them back? Because leaders are high achievers. Much of the literature states that it is because we doubt our accomplishments, however, I think it is because we are always so focused on getting better and doing more that we forget how far we have come. We literally forget to recognize our accomplishments.

What's even more is that we tend to focus on the negative and create more energy around it. There are times I replay a bad conversation or situation in my head over and over, wondering why I did something, wishing I would have said something different. Instead of doing this, we need to be very general around negative thoughts and let them go while at the same time trying to be very specific around the positive ones. The more you can internalize positive thoughts for clarity, the more it will become a natural practice to where you are always scanning for the positive.

This is the reason that a gratitude journal is such a cool gift to give yourself. Not only does it change your outlook from one of have-not

---

[10] Clance, P.R. & Imes, S. (1978). The impostor phenomenon in high achieving women: Dynamics and therapeutic intervention. *Psychotherapy: Theory, Research and Practice, 15,* 2410247.

to one of have, it also reminds you of those super important accomplishments. If you don't like taking the time to write, at least take five minutes before you go to sleep at night to be thankful for specific things that happened that day.

One way to battle imposter syndrome is to own your mistakes and verbalize them. When you share your mistakes, they start to lose their power over you. Remember my failed attempt at college? It had so much more power over me when I tried to hide it. However, I wasn't always this enlightened. It wasn't my idea to share it. But when I did, there was this magical phenomenon that people actually connected with me over it and showed support around it.

Here is what happened. While I was sitting on the Foundation board of directors, I applied for the position I now have with the hospital which is the Executive Director of the Foundation. I didn't get it due to my lack of education. To say I was embarrassed is a gross understatement. Not only was I embarrassed, I was frustrated and mortified. I would have to continue serving on that board, knowing that they knew that I wasn't good enough.

That embarrassment didn't begin to touch how I felt when the CEO of the hospital asked in front of the entire Hospital board of directors how I was doing on getting my degree. I hadn't shared with anyone that I was going back let alone that I had dropped out 20 years earlier. I wanted to crawl under the table, curl up in the fetal position and cry.

But later, as in just a few days, something started to happen. The more people found out about it, the more connections I made. People just like me started sharing their own regrets and missteps. They started telling about their own feelings of being inadequate. Then they started showing me understanding and support in ways I would never have imagined.

Eventually, I started to wear my mistake as a badge of honor. And it started to lose its power.

Plus, sharing it did something I could have never predicted. It prompted me to embrace my fear, face it head on and double down in my studies. I went back and finished my undergrad in a year and continued on to get my master's degree in ten months. I am convinced that the more we try to fight our fears and doubts, the bigger they will become. We truly have to become friends with them to see what they are trying to tell us and learn from them. If we don't, it will just build our self-doubt.

Self-doubt comes from our missteps. But if we aren't careful, it can easily become the cause of every new missed step in your life. Self-doubt steals dreams, denies hope, and assassinates faith. Let that stuff go. Share it with others. And then move on.

As you can imagine, awareness is just the tip of the iceberg. Knowing that our egos and our brains are wired like this is like having an extra weapon in your arsenal. Soon you will see those old thoughts for what they are: old news. I heard it described once as 'one thought thin'. I love this, because if you can get to a point where you dig deeper than that one thought, you will be halfway to the finish line. The rest of the journey will be so much easier. The more you practice choosing your thoughts intentionally, the easier it will get.

And that's the sweet spot, being able to notice quicker and quicker where you are holding yourself back, or more specifically, where your thoughts aren't serving you. Now that you know how to do this, it's time to get on to the fun part of rebuilding how you do want to think for yourself.

> **Key takeaway:**
>
> Notice where you say I'm not ready or I don't know. What are your triggers?

Chapter Eleven

RElabeling - Who do you love?

If you hear a voice within you say, you are not a painter, then by all means paint, and that voice will be silenced.

~ **Vincent Van Gogh**

We have now figured out what you want to think and why you want to think it in order to show up as only you can do. Now is the fun part of putting together how you will do it.

Have you ever noticed that most musicians don't start by singing their own music? They start by doing cover songs. This is a great way to begin the realization process of creating a new plan - your vision for your life and reconfiguring your labels and limiting beliefs. Think of people you would like to emulate and use that to guide how you want to show up.

If you were to emulate someone, who would it be?

Why do you want to be like them?

Can you see a pattern?

What could they do better?

What labels do you think they use to identify themselves?

Can you see using them for yourself?

If not, why?

As I stated earlier, there are aspirational core values (goals) and operational core values (your truth). Here is where we start to combine them.

Think about the Van Gogh quote at the beginning of this chapter. Look at your negative labels and thoughts and ask yourself:

1. Is that the truth?
2. How does that make me feel?
3. Is there any way I can turn this around?
4. Do I even want to?

When examining your life, take some time to ask yourself:

When did I form this belief?

What are some other interpretations of that belief?

Instead of saying I am not a runner, I need to get curious to say I choose not to run. Getting curious is a great tool that can only be implemented by being aware. Awareness is part of the M&Ms technique of leadership that I teach: Mindfulness, Mindset and Mind Management. They all go hand in hand because finding a new label is not enough if you don't believe you can ever achieve it. You have to be able to detect your negative thought patterns and see where they sabotage you.

Brooke Castillo is someone I want to emulate. She teaches other coaches how to manage their own minds and help others do the same. She teaches what she calls the Model. I have seen this in many other forms by other teachers and authors, but I think the Model is the easiest to use and captures everything to make it the most effective tool.

The Model is a very simple tool to use to detect what we are thinking about something to determine if it is helping us or hindering us. It helps us to identify feelings, emotions, and energy that we are attaching to our thoughts. It works like this: in life there are circumstances. Whatever happens in our life (the circumstance) triggers a thought. Many times, we have a feeling that is attached to that thought. This drives the actions we take which creates the results we see. The acronym is CTFAR.

To use the Model, you need to take time to recognize your thoughts. Using awareness from the previous chapters, take some time to notice your thoughts about any area that seems to bothering you. For any area of your life you want to improve, start by journaling your thoughts about that area.

For instance, before I started listening to Brooke's podcast The Life Coach School and learned about the Model, I wanted to lose 10 pounds. There were so many thoughts I had about this including:

- I'm too busy.
- I've tried and failed before.
- Losing weight is hard.
- It's not fair that I can't eat what I want.

Now you plug those thoughts into the T line of the model below.

- ❖ C - Circumstances are facts that are neutral. (I want to lose 10 pounds.)
- ❖ T - Thoughts are what we think about that circumstance. (Losing weight is hard.)
- ❖ F - Feelings are what that thought creates in me. (Frustrated, sad, defeated)
- ❖ A - Actions are the result of those thoughts and feelings. (I continue to eat because I am justified and think it is so hard or feel that what I'm doing is not going to help.)
- ❖ R - Results - (I don't lose any weight.)

This process is in some ways similar to what Byron Katie teaches called The Work. Remember in chapter 7 when I mentioned the question - Is that the truth? The Work is based upon that opening question. If you are experiencing a thought that is causing you pain, examine that thought by asking yourself if it is the truth.

When doing this you need to remember that feelings and emotions are not bad nor good. They are data and energy to help us adapt to perceived opportunities and threats. We need to use them as a resource to do better, think better and act better. The Work and the Model are tools that help you recognize negative thought patterns and more importantly the beliefs that are behind the thoughts. They can also help you plug in positive thoughts or at least alternative ones in for the negative ones. Quite simply, beliefs create results. When you believe that you can lose weight, your thoughts support you and drive the actions that create the results you want. The key is to see when your thoughts aren't supporting your big dreams and goals.

Take my friend Jane who found herself so stuck in her circumstances, in her thinking that she couldn't find a way out. The story is that she had moved to our small community in a very rural part of Nebraska to help out her best friend open a store. However, she didn't realize or seem to take into account that she would be 11 to 12 hours by vehicle away from her kids which didn't seem like a big deal until grand-babies started to appear. Family always changes the dynamic, right?

This is a prime example of how your values can change over time, and just like that, a new grand-baby can totally change what you value. A sick parent who you may have to take care of or one that is having health issues, may change a value in some sort of small way that fits into a bigger value. Your bigger value is probably family, but maybe it's been on the back burner for career or location or job opportunity and then something happens and it shifts. For me it was having my son. Suddenly, work life balance seemed to be a thing. Everything had changed. This led to a big rethink in order to get clear again on what I valued.

Getting back to Jane. She was so stuck in what she was thinking about that she couldn't see there was any other way out. There was no winning for her. What I want to pose here is that there is always a way to win. There is always a way around something. I refer to it as using the back door. It is amazing how innovative you can become when your back is up against the wall. But oftentimes, decisions such as this keep us stuck because we feel we have no options, no choices.

Take for instance if you thought you were stuck in a dead-end job. In all reality - you are choosing to work where you are. Choosing to feed your family and put gas in your car. Choosing to continue to get a paycheck. These are things you should feel proud of, not stuck.

With Jane, I started talking with her about what it was that was holding her back. It was the usual suspects. That she didn't have enough money and she would need to sell her house and get a job. There were many reasons, all of which were valid. However, what one person sees as a valid reason, another sees as an excuse. It is so much easier to see excuses for what they are when we are on the outside looking in. Think about those family members or friends who frustrate you with their stories, when it is so clear to you what they need to do, what they need to try. However, from the inside, we can't see it. And even when we do, we don't want to believe it.

Think of your friends that are using the same excuses over and over. To them they are very valid reasons. So, what I am posing to you is that you have very valid reasons. You do. Perhaps you want to lose weight but your husband loves a home cooked meal and he always wants bread and pasta and you have little kids at home to feed. You wouldn't want to cook a whole different meal for yourself and you can't pose your new obscene healthy choices on them, can you?

I get it, I've been there, I wrote the script. I now pick up fast food for my husband and son and come home and make a salad. The looks they give me are not always friendly. But they know I am doing it because I want to be healthier. So, what are your excuses? More importantly, what are your thoughts that are holding you back?

Jane's thoughts were that she couldn't do that. She couldn't pick up and move on her own. Her thought was that she didn't have enough money. She also didn't want to upset her friend. However, her thoughts had serious feelings attached to them that was creating the miserable state she found herself in. Getting her to recognize her thoughts for what they were took some work, but with the Model, we were able to break down the feelings that were causing her inaction.

Finally, I asked her the question that changed it all. If she could be extremely happy and successful in either place, without any ramifications, which would she choose? This is a powerful question to ask yourself when you get to a major crossroad. It works because it gets you past your limiting beliefs and the negative feelings that you attach to your thoughts. For Jane, she finally chose to sell her house, pack up her life and move closer to her family.

We have to get out of our own way. We have to question our thinking. Just by becoming aware we put some distance between our true selves and those thoughts that are not serving us.

I know how hard this is, believe me. I get caught up in my own vicious thought cycle all of the time. Yet the practices outlined in the next few chapters will help make it easier.

Key takeaway:

Who do you admire and why? What about them would you like to emulate? Practice that.

Chapter Twelve

Mindfulness & Choosing a new response

Between stimulus and response, there is a space. In that space is our power to choose our response. IN our response lies our freedom.

~ **Viktor E. Frankl**

Mindfulness, mindset and mind-management are the holy triad of becoming authentic and effective. They are the key to conquering the busyness that has become an epidemic.

Mindfulness is not necessarily meditation. I just want to get this out of the way because I have seen many people cringe when I talk about being mindful. Mindfulness really means being present in the current moment. It is the key to the door. The door that gives you freedom. The door that is your entrance into all the possibility of happiness, potential and resiliency.

Using mindfulness will help you see the neutrality of circumstances. When you get to a place of where you are present to see thoughts that your mind is experiencing, you will be able to keep yourself out of the emotional dust storm that can ensue when we get married to our thoughts. Have you ever been in charge of an initiative or a project and started to get married to your thoughts? Did you start to dig in your heels and think "it had better be my way or the highway!"?

When we do this, we can get very judgmental which can send us into our own downward spiral funk. The key is to be aware enough that you can catch yourself in a thought that is separating you from the neutral reality of the situation. More importantly, we need to realize when we are in this emotional state that we need to just sit with the feelings and not do anything rash.

For example, one of the initiatives I was in charge of at work was bringing on a customer service consulting company. As the point person it would be very easy to think it needs to be my way or the highway. I found myself in that position many times. From naming the initiative to choosing the speakers to determining how it would be rolled out. But each time the thing that saved me from getting really sideways with myself and the other people involved was when I took time to pause and question and think about what the big picture was. In a word, I was practicing being mindful.

So many times, we lose track of the fact that circumstances are neutral. We are deep in the forest and we can't even see it because there's just trees all around us. Like the proverbial goldfish in the water, we need to be able to see when the water is our thoughts and we are biased in our thinking.

In simple terms, mindfulness is the ability to see with clarity, free from habitual ways of thinking and reacting. And even though it's simple, this is not easy. It takes intentionality.

In order to be intentional, we need to mind the gap that Viktor is mentioning in the quote at the beginning of this chapter. This takes being mindful and present. To notice when we are about to do something that is not in line with what we want to accomplish or how we want to show up.

It is for this very reason that creating new habits in our thinking can be extremely helpful.

Think about when you get stressed out at work and the first thing you want to do is run back to your desk and shovel in a whole mouthful of candy. It's your thought that led you to a mouthful of peanut M&Ms, not the circumstances.

Or how about this, do you find yourself assuming the worst in yourself? When you are unsure of others, do you automatically jump to why they may not like you or that you may have offended them? Jill recently moved into a new neighborhood. She had been trying to get together with a neighbor and had to reschedule. Later in the week when they were supposed to get together she got the following text.

"Looking back at our chat history, getting together isn't looking too good."

She automatically jumped to the thought that she must have offended her new neighbor when she had to reschedule. To any outsider, this text is pretty benign. But when you are in the middle of a situation where you want to be liked and fit in, you start to overanalyze everything. You start looking for reasons that support your thinking even if the thinking is way off base.

So where do you find yourself overanalyzing? What do you want your new thought and your new response to be? Practice your new thoughts, patterns and responses. Deliberately put yourself in situations that will try your new skill.

Underneath it all are core beliefs that mesh with our thoughts to keep creating those behaviors that are not serving us well.

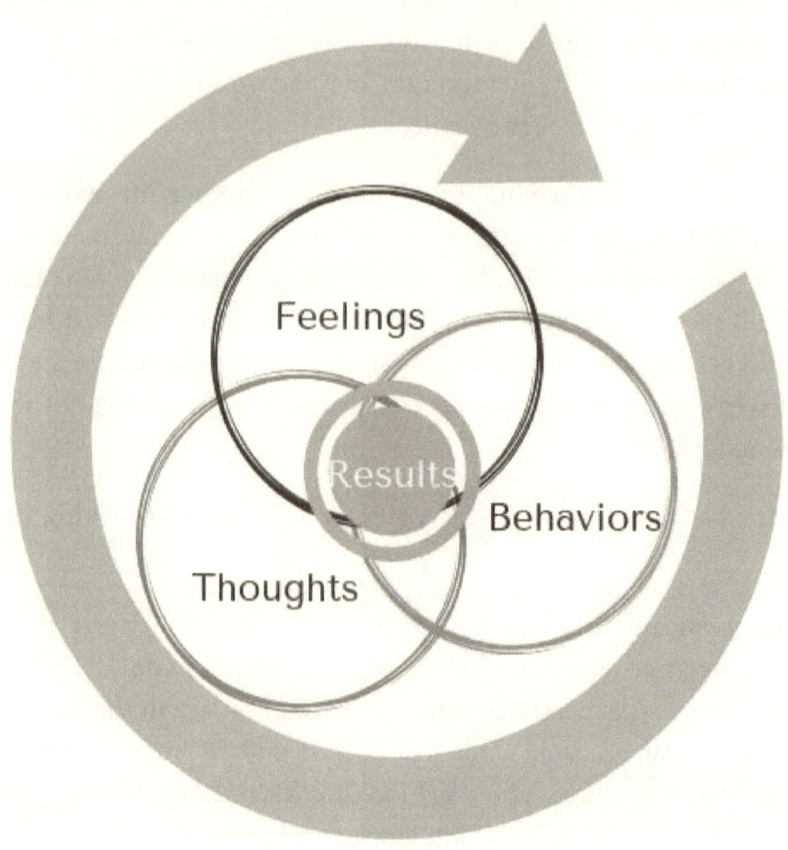

To develop your new response, answer these questions:

Do you hate conflict?

Do you hate making people uncomfortable?

Are you afraid of being judged by others?

What is your pattern? Do you choose immediate comfort over prolonged progress towards your goal? Do you eat something sweet and sugary now, which sabotages your diet and your long-term goal?

Or how about the times you automatically take on extra work just because someone asks you to?

Try to find those triggers we discussed earlier and think of the new way you want to show up and then set up your environment to support you. Once that is done, take the time to craft responses before you make them. Take full advantage of the gap and make it work for you.

And then practice, practice, practice.

If you slip into old patterns, whether they are thoughts or actions, don't beat yourself up. Keep working at it. Eventually it will get easier. Soon you will become more resilient and be able to snap back to intention sooner rather than later.

Becoming aware is a practice. Simple in concept yet sometimes difficult to implement. The practice itself isn't hard, but you do have to take time for it. Let me show you an example.

Think about a person, a time, an instance - when you have felt wronged.

Take a moment here and really feel it.

Here is one of my examples. One night when, while getting ready for bed, I noticed a new DVD on the dresser. It was a movie I hadn't heard of. I asked my husband what it was about. In an incredulous and snarky tone, he went on to state how it was the recipient of all the awards of the season - Oscar, Golden Globe, etc.

"Did I live under a rock for crying out loud?"

Needless to say, my first reaction was hurt. I was upset and felt unloved. It took me a few moments (oh who am I kidding, it took me until morning) to realize that I didn't want to react with tears. I didn't want to be pissy. In my heart, I know those responses are not true to me. And in all reality, I could really care less about the movie.

I was just trying to create conversation. The next morning, I told him that. I shared how it made me feel and that by acting the way he did makes me want to close up. However, I am not that person. So, while I won't shut down completely, I won't be asking him any questions about his interests. His response was being sorry. However, had I blown up at him (my first gut reaction) he would have dug in and been a bigger butt head.

So now, back to you: take some time and think of a situation of your own. How did it make you feel?

How do you feel right now remembering it?

How do you feel in your stomach, in your chest, in your head?

What thoughts were (are) running through your head?

Now, going back to the time - How did you react?

Knowing what you do about being able to choose your response, one that is in alignment with who you are and who you want to be, how will you craft your response for next time?

Think about the trigger points. The buttons that the other person pushes to get a certain response out of you. We all do this, conscious or not. We say and do certain things in our relationships, knowing that the other person will respond in a certain way.

I have a few friends that have gone through divorces. In each case, one spouse will inevitably raise the bar when pushing the buttons. When they don't get the response they are used to, they will escalate their demands and their tactics. Dr. Harriet Lerner calls this the *Dance of Anger*. The longer your history with that person, the stronger the dance. This is why it is extremely difficult to stop these patterns with siblings or parents whom we have had relationships for decades.

What trigger points happened in the situation you thought about earlier?

This is where you can use the awareness gap to identify opportunities. It is also where you combine your core values (that are true to where you operate) with your intentions (that are aspirational).

What new response can you start to practice?

If it helps, think of someone in your life who you are extremely close with, someone who you would trust to always have your well-being at heart. What if that person were to tell you something that felt like a true criticism? How would you take it? Would you be able to see the intent behind the criticism? Can you keep this in mind to create your new response and actions for others which you trust less? Remember that our go-to thoughts create go-to actions. Meaning we will continue to react in habitual ways until we put some intent into changing them.

Take Susan for instance. Susan has worked her way up through the healthcare system. She started as a tech in school, worked her way through nursing, got her masters and now is the senior director of nursing in a regional hospital. Recently, this journey has catapulted Susan from floor manager to the senior director in just over a year. Susan has went from managing a floor to directing four floors. She is no longer a manager but a leader of leaders. This is a big mindset adjustment for many. Susan came to me one day, beaming, exclaiming, "Did you see that?!?" I just told a charge nurse that she is the leader on this floor. I asked her what she was going to do to handle her issue. I said okay, go do it. That it was her job and she no longer needs to come to me for approval." She went on to say, "I did it. I delegated and it saved me at least 20 minutes."

What Susan doesn't know is that it saved her way more than 20 minutes. It will have prevented hours of putting out fires in the future.

But it wasn't always easy for Susan. Her go-to thought was to fix whatever problem is brought to her. Normally, she would have jumped up and gone to save the day. This is another whole issue that managers bring on themselves, the martyr syndrome, that keeps us in the busyness tornado.

Through many discussions, Susan was open to feedback because she trusted the intent behind the conversation. Her decision to become a leader of leaders called for her to create new responses. New responses are the foundation for showing up. However, showing up is a continuous journey. It isn't just a once and done type of thing. It does require hard work and doesn't happen overnight. Sure, you can make up your mind to do something different and succeed the next day only to wear out from the exhaustion of something new. New thoughts are tiring for the brain. Our brains like to stay comfortable, thinking old thoughts. Therefore, showing up takes practice. Some days you will fail and some days you will fly. Some days it is so hard, but at the end of those days are when you should be the proudest.

Always be brave.

Be daring enough to embrace your vulnerabilities.

Creating new responses takes courage and time, patience and practice. You probably won't get it right for a couple of times. Just as I had to stop and breathe and form a new response in the bedroom with my husband that night, you do to.

It may take many times of stumbling before you get it right. And it will be frustrating. There will be times when it is just easier to play the dance. But those small wins when you do get it right, when you are true to yourself, to the core you, to your soul - are so worth it.

When you make a practice of this, the end benefit will be your resiliency time and rebound time. Much like an Olympic Swimmer who keeps trying to shave a second off of their time, you are doing the same. It is a skill to hone and practice.

Becoming aware is the first step. Realizing what is going on. Watching your life as a spectator. Noticing how you act and react. You will soon begin to notice where your words, your thoughts and your actions are no longer serving you and how you need to create your responses.

The present moment is the field on which the game of life happens.

~ Eckhart Tolle

For this reason, mini meditations - or times of mindfulness - are very effective for creating awareness and new thoughts.

Aside from the many health benefits of meditation (reducing anxiety, stress, irritability & blood pressure), it also starts to create neural pathways - or new ways to connect thoughts. By practicing new responses instead of being in reactionary mode all of the time, you will actually start to carve new paths in your brain helping you retain and implement your new response - making it easier and easier to be the true remarkable you.

Dan Harris has a great book and app called 10% Happier. In it, he describes his own personal quest for purpose and alignment. He also breaks it down to this, meditation may not be the end all, be all- but it can definitely make us 10% happier.

Many books have been written on meditation. But that's not the purpose here. What I want us to do here is use the main principles of meditation to become aware of where our lives are not really ours. You don't have to do formal, sit down, palms up, crisscross applesauce seating, chanting ummmmmmmmm, to realize the benefits of meditation. You don't even have to call it meditation.

I prefer to think of it as stopping, becoming aware and being present.

Our purpose here for meditation is to build points of awareness into our lives so that we may recognize when we are not acting on purpose.

Dan's steps go like this:

1. Recognize- just acknowledge your thought, your feeling. Just admit to it.
2. Allow - lean into it. Let it be.
3. Investigate - how is this affecting your body.
4. Non-Identification - for example, realizing that feeling angry does not make you angry. It is just a passing state of mind.

Being mindful is especially useful when we may not be in the right mindset. When you are in a funky frame of mind, or are being crunchy as my sister calls it, the quickest way back to neutral is to start questioning things. The only way you will know to question is if you are being mindful.

You can use questioning (like Byron's 'Is it the truth?') in any situation you find yourself -from the everyday situations like being cut off in traffic (perhaps they were on the way *to* the hospital and didn't intentionally cut you off) to a mom letting her kids run rampant in your store (perhaps they are on their way home *from* the hospital) to a person who appears to ignore you, being downright rude (perhaps they are going *through* cancer treatments that aren't working.) This will help you see that there might be other reasons for a circumstance than the ones you had assumed.

You can also use the Model. Say someone does cut you off. The circumstance is that they cut you off. The thought could be "Hmmmm they must really be in a hurry, poor things." Or it could be "Wow! What jerks they are for cutting me off." Just realize that whatever thought you pick, it is bound to bring up some sort of feeling and all of it is optional.

Regardless of what you use, realize that a thought is harmless. It is the belief we attach to it that creates all of our suffering. As Byron states it, "A belief is a thought that we have been attaching to, usually for years."

The purpose for analyzing our thoughts, our judgments, is to ask ourselves "Is it the truth?"

It is most definitely our version of the truth.

But is ours the only version?

Think about it, disagreements stem from different perceptions creating different realities.

However, there is one universal truth. No matter how well we know another person, we don't know what they are going through at any given moment. This practice helps us slow down and give them the benefit of the doubt.

So, use questions to ask yourself if there may be another perspective to the story. The story that you are telling yourself. The story that you have kept alive. If you are having a problem getting distance from your story, ask a trusted friend to give you their perspective. I am always amazed at how two people can see and hear the same thing and walk away with such different takes on the situation. Then use this perspective to create your new response.

The practice of using mindfulness (moments to become aware) and combining it with mindset (your perspective and becoming curious as to other perspectives) is necessary for a new response. Understanding is part of the creating process. It will get easier and better when you are using a growth mindset.

> **Key takeaway:**
>
> Remember that we never know where someone is coming from, going through or going to. Be mindful.

Chapter Thirteen

Mindset & Why training is important

Once your mindset changes, everything on the outside will change along with it.

~Steve Maraboli

In her groundbreaking book *Mindset,* Carol Dweck explains the difference between a fixed mindset and growth mindset. The main premise is that people that believe they can grow and develop their abilities do better in school and in life.[11]

As a recovering P3, it was hard for me to realize that I do not have to be perfect at something the first time that I do it. While there is much freedom in knowing this, there are still times my brain forgets and starts nagging me with fear and criticism that what I do must be a success and that in order to be considered a success, it must be perfect.

Guess what this type of thinking leads to? You got it, procrastination. For people who suffer from busyness, procrastination is like a heavy weight dragging us down. We need to remember that there is always a chance to do better. Look at technology. There is always a newer, latest and greatest version

---

[11] Dweck, C. S. (2017). *Mindset. The new psychology of success.* London: Robinson, an imprint of Little, Brown Book Group.

coming out. The same is true for you. Your growth and development will come in each of these versions.

There is no one blueprint, plan, or map. You have to write your own. That's the part that's hard. But that's also the part that liberates you, freeing you from the molds of shoulds and have-tos.

By now you have the bones necessary to create that map. Lucky for you, the map can be tweaked as many times as necessary in order to start to feel like it is truly representational of who you are.

For this reason alone, practice is necessary. But practice alone won't get you to living a life that is effective and authentic to you. It does no good to practice something that isn't tested or that won't get you the results you want or heaven forbid, is the total wrong way to go about it.

Take my son for instance, who has earnestly taken up golf in the past year. Before that, he did some small golf clinics but for the most part, he has learned from my husband and me. And let me tell you, we are not pros! Poor Cameron has picked up some BAD habits. The biggest being that he swings a golf club like a bat. This can be great for distance but horrible for accuracy. Even if you aren't familiar with golf, accuracy is king. Especially when playing on courses that have wild land grasses all around that house rabbit holes and rattle snakes. Needless to say, Cam has lost several golf balls this year. The good part is that he is practicing more than ever. The bad part, as you may have guessed already, is that he has been practicing the wrong techniques. The key is for him to find a new way to swing the golf club.

The same is true for your life. Just as Cam's coach will have to break some bad habits, you will too.

You have to practice your new thinking and responses, for those are what create your actions and in turn your results.

The only way you will ever find out if something is working for you is to try it, feel it, live it and breathe it. Your gut will tell you when you have made a wrong move. Or the situation will just like Cameron's lost balls have shown him. But you have to be willing to listen to it which as you saw earlier means making time for whitespace, time for reflection and time for renewing your vow and promise to yourself to be authentically you.

In the workplace, we call this the PDSA cycle: plan, do, study, act. While many of us know this to be the logical course of action for the workplace and processes that happen there, we don't feel it is necessary to use the same un-objective study of our own lives and our own thinking.

This is because we have developed programming over the years that has been ingrained in us by decades of thoughts. Plus, many times we will find ourselves in autopilot mode when it comes to our thinking.

Whatever you fight, you strengthen, and what you resist, persists.

~Eckhart Tolle

This book has hopefully created the curiosity in you to examine your thoughts, motives, mindsets and actions. You need to choose your emotional disc with intent. Don't let the subject at hand be the reason for choosing your emotional disc. Remember to use the Model and that all circumstances are neutral. This is instrumental in getting you to a place where you can explore.

When a true emotional funk sets in, how do you get through it to the other side? This is what is the key. **You must go through it.** So many of us are in a constant battle with our emotions. Trying to ward them off to stay positive. I know this, because that is me. At times, I feel myself (my brain) wanting to slip right back into the position of ignoring the issue, because this is easier, because it is like an old pair of sweat pants, worn and comfy and oh so inviting.

Our brains like the familiar. They like to conserve energy and more importantly, they like to stay safe. But this work takes energy. It takes conscious thought to actually change which is the hardest piece of the whole puzzle. There will be times where it will suck. You may find yourself wondering:

"Why does this continue to be so hard?!"

"Why do I continue to find myself in these situations where I am REACTING?!"

"I know this is just a result of my thoughts, so why can't I seem to pull myself out of this funk?!"

"I teach this stuff for crying out loud! Why can't I be better at it?!"

"I just want to feel sorry for myself for a little bit!"

These are all perfectly normal. So, if you find yourself in this place, don't panic. It's actually amazing how aware you are in this very moment!

This isn't something you learn about, implement the next minute and then "Ta-da!", you have a new life. No, quite the contrary my friend. This is something that is like every other thing in life, it takes work and practice and more work and more practice. It is an evolution. But it is so worth it! This is a big deal!

When you are experiencing thoughts like the ones above, feel them. Work your way through them and let them wash through you. A good practice for working through them is to journal about them. I finally gave into the journaling craze about 15 years ago when I read Julia Cameron's *The Artist's Way*.

I call it a craze because my thoughts at the time were that it was just plain silly. I mean, C'mon, who has the time to journal anyhow? But once I researched the importance of whitespace and then read her book, I was hooked.

In it, she talks about journaling in a way that seemed to speak to my soul. She created a practice where she writes as fast as she possibly can for three full pages and does this religiously as a practice every single day. In the book she tells of how writing like this helped to heal her for she actually used the practice to vent and get all of her furies out of her head.

There is something truly liberating about cleansing the mind in this manner. It allows you to vent, and dissect and analyze your thoughts. And then this magic happens. Your mind starts to move on. It is a glorious feeling that helps you back to the right mindset that you can continue to grow.

So, realize that you will screw up. Be graceful with yourself. As a leader, I always teach other leaders to use kindness and grace. What I mean is that many conversations we must have are crucial and we need to remember that no matter how much we don't like the behavior of someone, they are still a person, a human being. We need to remember the same thing with ourselves. Our egos are fragile creatures that have many responsibilities. They need to be recognized for their awesomeness all the while they are trying to protect us from harm and danger. This is how it is supposed to work. You will not be perfect. But you will get better over time. You will get to a place where it doesn't take as long, where you can snap back quicker and truly start to build resiliency.

> *I haven't failed, I found 10,000 solutions that didn't work.*
>
> ~ **Thomas Edison**

The work is supposed to be hard. It is supposed to suck. You are supposed to feel this way. There will be a valley for every hill you climb.

We always want things to be easier. We want to be happier. To feel better. This is why the grass is always greener somewhere else.

If you think it is easier for someone else or better somewhere else, guess again. Do you ever look at people who have lost a bunch of weight and think, "Well of course they could do it. They have a better metabolism than me. Their spouse doesn't expect a four-course meal every night with comfort foods like mashed potatoes and gravy."

We always think the grass is greener and easier to mow somewhere else.

Let me tell you, I have fantasized about it all. I think if I lived in Europe, life would be blissful. I would never have to deal with crappy weather, windstorms, or rude people. All of the sudden I would be able to get to my goal weight and my job would be joyous every single day. In these fantasies, sometimes my family is with me and quite frankly, sometimes they are not.

You can change the scenario and the words, but the GIG (grass is greener) scenario is true for every person and even organizations. In healthcare, we get graded by patients who fill out surveys. The results are reported in the form of HCAHPS (the Hospital Consumer Assessment of Healthcare Providers and Systems). Many hospitals will give all sorts of excuses as to why their scores aren't as high as their peers. Things like our patients have more social issues, they are higher acuity (sicker), Mid-Westerners don't rate anything as excellent, our people are overworked, etc.

The same mindset could be found in small business. I had a business owner once tell me that our community doesn't support small business. That they buy everything online and we just weren't big enough to be viable. Yet another owner of a small salon increased her footprint and number of stylists from 3 to 30 in just a matter of years.

The problem in most of these scenarios is our mindset. It is why some don't accept failure as an option. Because after all, failure just means some iteration didn't work or that you gave up before getting it figured out. We quote Thomas Edison all of the time, but think it doesn't apply to us. We don't give ourselves grace to find 10,000 solutions that didn't work.

Failure is just a label we give something. Do you think the iPhone 4 was a failure? I mean at the time of this writing, we are up to the iPhone 8 and iPhone X. In product development, there is always the opportunity for a new and improved version, a 2.0, 3.0 and on and on. It's called iteration and I think as humans we forget that life is indeed a journey and that we just need to keep working on our iterations and improvements. But in the meantime, there will be times of suck. Just as there will be times of awesome. And it is supposed to be that way! This is why I call it creating a map because the journey is never ending. Oh, but it does get easier and sweeter if you just hang in there.

Think about a diet. So many people view a diet as a pass/fail. What if we just thought of it as a new version of how we take care of ourselves? I have never been super fit, skinny or in shape. However, I have pretty much been able to stay at a healthy average weight. Since reaching the big mid-life mark, I have realized that my version of eating and exercise has needed to continually be tweaked. At first I quit diet Coke. It wasn't easy because there were times I still craved it. But just knowing that there are times I will be having those cravings, that they are just normal and a function of my mind, and that YES, they are supposed to suck, makes it easier to let all of that just wash through me.

So what are you going through that sucks? Is it supposed to be part of the process? Think about an Olympic athlete going through training. Do you think they are saying to themselves, "This is too hard. It shouldn't be this hard." I am doubting it. I don't personally know any Olympic hopefuls, but I am guessing that they realize hard work is all part of the process. Maybe you don't want to deal with the hard work. That is perfectly acceptable. But then realize it for what it is and reset your goals.

However, if you feel that whatever it is that you want out of life, whether it be a skinnier bod or happier marriage, is worth the work, then also realize that sometimes the work sucks. Accept it. Get over it and move on. Have the courage to honor the commitment to yourself.

"Without courage, we cannot practice any other virtue with any consistency. We can't be kind, true, merciful, generous or honest."

~ Maya Angelou

Start acting as if. Ask yourself, "How would a healthy person eat? How would my future self tell me to eat?" and listen to that voice.

In order for things to change you have to see them as you want them to be. You can't keep looking at your history to create your future. You won't find any evidence there to support what you need to do.

Think about the things you have made happen in your life: little or big. Setting an alarm clock means you will get to your interview on time. Setting you up for a new job. Perhaps one that you thought you would never get. You can use this to look at anything you have done in your life, big or small. Thoughts create reality. And then realize that your new reality will take some work. There will be some hills and valleys and that is okay.

A thought = a point of attraction. Regardless if it's an observation of current reality or it's a vision brought upon by imagination. The universe doesn't hear what you say, it hears what you feel, your vibrational energy. Remember that you can grow from everything so keep a good mindset by choosing good thoughts.

> **Key takeaway:**
>
> Life is only as good as your mindset. Look at everything as an opportunity to learn and grow.

Chapter Fourteen

That's not me

Perhaps you have gotten this far and think it's not that bad. That you aren't that person. You know. The person who can't see the forest for the trees. If that's the case, then you are past the trees my dear. You are in the weeds. There has to be a reason you chose this book. Something about the title or cover spoke to you. So, let's take a minute and see if any of this does pertain to you.

Do you go from meeting to meeting to meeting?
Do you take at least three hours a week to think about the things you want to accomplish?
Do you focus on the big picture or the minute details?
Do you let others do their jobs?
Do you constantly check everyone else's work?
Do you just do things yourself because it is quicker than telling someone else how to do it?
Do you go to every meeting you are invited to?
Do you attend every meeting that your subordinates run/hold?
Are you included in way too many group emails?
Do you feel that most people aren't doing their jobs as good as you could?
Do you check every piece of work of your team members?
Does your team experience high turnover?
Have you become a bottleneck because all things must come through you?
How long does it take you to respond to high priority emails?
Do over half of your emails come to you as high priority?

Do you find that you are the only one speaking at your team meetings?

Have your team members become blasé about their jobs or work?

If you answered mostly with yes, you may be micromanaging which is a big issue to face when trying to conquer busyness.

There is a difference between being detail oriented and micromanaging. You can notice the details of anything you look at or focus on without needing to approve every single thing the people who report to you are doing.

According to Jim Schleckser of CEO, Inc., great CEOs understand the need and power that comes from delegation. In order to get more things done, they use the 70% rule to delegate. If any person of their team can do a task at least 70% as well as they can, they delegate it.[12] Of the many managers, directors and leaders I work with, I have found that at least 40-50% of the routine task work they are doing could be delegated.

When team members become disengaged or blasé it is because they feel what they are doing doesn't matter anyhow. That you will pick it apart or redo it anyhow so why even bother.

To get yourself out of this horrible spot you have found yourself in, focus on the theme song of Frozen with me, and "Let it Go."

Use your abilities as a catalyst for change.

Whether in an organization or running your own business, recognize your strengths and work with them. High achieving people have a real problem with this idea because that would mean

---

[12] Schleckser, J. (2014, August 14). The 70 Percent Rule--When to Delegate. Retrieved from *https://www.inc.com/jim-schleckser/the-70-rule-when-to-delegate.html*

letting someone else take on the things they are not so good at or don't enjoy.

This sounds silly. I know. But think about it. Do you find times when you say things like, "It would be quicker to just do it myself"? That is the hard part of delegation. In order for someone to make your life easier, we have to teach them what we need. We also need to teach them to do it in a way that we can accept and work with.

This is delegation 101. While it can be excruciating in the beginning it is so worth it once you get that person up to speed. And the beauty of it is, if you are open minded, they may figure out a way to do it better than you ever even imagined.

Take my friend Missy who owned a business for years. She found it hard to hire help that had the 'design' eye she did. When she dressed her mannequins and made up her displays, items sold like hotcakes. When her staff did it, they never quite had the same success. Nor was the feel of what they were doing what she wanted for her store. She found herself in quite the pickle because she didn't have enough time to do the displays because the ever-mounting administrative duties of book-keeping, ordering, etc. had started to consume her life. Soon she was looking to hire a bookkeeper as well. After a coaching call, it became quite clear that she would rather do the floor work of creating displays and working with customers than do the back-end work of administrative duties.

The answer became obvious that it would be easier and better for her to hire a bookkeeper instead of a sales person. However, it wasn't as easy as that. Even though Missy could see this, she felt she needed to hold onto the accounting. That she needed to control it. Most small business owners are used to doing everything on their own. It is hard to let go of the reigns in even a small area of their baby that they have brought created. If this is you, start small in your delegation and work your way up.

What are some baby steps you could take? What is one small thing you could give to someone else to do?

Are there clear directions you can give them to do it?

You need to start to loosen the reigns. Start first with the delegation rule mentioned above. Then gradually build up the trust of your team. Start to let them try and do things on their own. They will fail. Know this. But think about the times you have truly learned the most. Did it come from easy success or tough challenges? I can tell you that the things that have stayed with me the most came from learning things the hard way.

If you want them to fail faster, test them a bit. I had a brilliant general manager who taught me the ropes very quickly. My first week into management, she said that the soda machine wasn't working. I went and poked and prodded and found nothing. She asked me what I was going to do. I said I guess I would call the repair man to come and fix it. Mind you, this would cost a few hundred bucks just for them to step foot in our store. She asked if I was sure I wanted to do that, if I had truly checked everything.

After looking again, I still determined that a repair man needed to be called. That's when she showed me that she had turned off the power switch on the back of the machine. This was a crash course lesson in critical thinking/problem solving 101. For someone who was not so mechanically inclined, this was gold.

It did not, however, feel like it at the time. But guess what, 30 years later and it is still one of my most vivid management memories. Most people learn from doing. Let your people do. Let them try and fail. If you give them the opportunity, they may try and succeed. This takes time on the front end but pays huge dividends on the back end in the form of empowering them, making them feel valued and giving you back your time and give you the time for working on YOU. It will give you freedom to pull away from all those tasks that suck up your time and energy.

You are meant for the big picture items. Don't play small by staying in the weeds. For most new leaders, micromanagement is their Achilles heel. They are used to doing the tasks and processes that got them noticed and poised for management. It is a huge mindset shift to realize that your strength lies in pulling away from the weeds, not staying in them. And while the weeds are comfortable, they are what's holding you back.

Managing your mind.

To delegate effectively - we need people to do their jobs right. More than that, we need to keep our cool when things go south. We need to practice emotional intelligence. All of this thought work is doing just that. The more you manage your mind, the more neutral you will become. This is where effective people live.

In order to create quicker resiliency, you must start to build processes to put in place when you feel triggered. For instance, when you get so mad you can't see straight, go take a walk. Breathe for a count of ten breaths. Close your eyes and visualize. Do whatever it takes to stop the swirling of thoughts and emotions taking place in your brain and body. Whatever you do, don't hit send on that vicious email, or whatever other bad action you are about to take.

Take for instance this experience I had. I was in a job where my boss had put me in charge of growing the dues membership of our organization. This was fine as I truly believed more people needed our services and knew we could create better relationships. However, after being there for a year, I was starting to realize there were politics at play, bridges to mend, and egos in place that would make this much more difficult than I had previously imagined. Still, I was in it to win it and working hard to make that happen. Until one day I found out that he hadn't been billing for the memberships and services we currently had in place. This infuriated me. I had been working with a client for nine months and they hadn't been billed for any of my services. As you can imagine, this sent many mixed messages and I felt it made me look foolish when I had been in conversations about dues and fees with some of these very people. I was instantly upset.

Now I don't know about you, but when I get this type of angry, my mind starts making irrational threats. Threats like, "I'll show him. I'll quit and then where will he be with his almighty dues?" Perhaps you have thought similar things when fighting with a loved one. For some reason, my thoughts usually turn to flights of fancy - ones where I flee the scene to move on to greener pastures. In fact, this is a normal response for most people.

The point for now is to create that action or as we call it in the medical business 'hard-stop' to put into place for when you are feeling like this. Something that will make you stop and reimplement the gap that will give you the space to act with intention.

What can you do that will remind you to take a quick time-out?

Is there a phrase you can say, a thought you can summon, or a tiny action you can implement?

For me, it is the power of the pause. To take 20 seconds and say nothing, do nothing, and just sit. But when I am heated, this isn't always reality. Sometime I do have to walk it off. I have to admit that I am not great about saying, "You know, I am not in a great space at the moment. Can I take 5 and come back to this conversation?" However, I have seen it in action and it really does work.

The more we can do this, the better we will feel. Because we will find empowerment, grace and neutrality in these moments. And that makes it worth it.

> **Key takeaway:**
>
> Delegate to stay out of the weeds. You are meant for bigger things.

Chapter Fifteen

TIP: *Give yourself a break*

Busy is not a status symbol. You are not always meant to grind through it.

When you find yourself in the middle of big ol' shit storm (as we say in the Midwest), internally, let it ride. Don't do anything or make any decisions. Just be. Or better yet do something that feels good or makes you feel productive. For me, it is cleaning and organizing junk drawers. Something about tossing out crap, organizing chaos and scrubbing away the grime makes me feel about 125% better.

Knowing that this too shall pass is one of the hardest things for me to recognize. We all know that failures and disappointments are good for growth, but that doesn't make them any easier to swallow. So be supportive of yourself. I like to say supportive instead of gentle because being gentle with myself would feel like an almost 180 degree turn from where I usually find myself. If this is you too, at least agree to be supportive.

Give yourself advice that you would give to a close friend. And LISTEN. Listen to that advice. If it is too much to ask to get to a place of gratitude, then at least get to a place of nothingness. Make no decisions, do no big tasks, just be.

Realize that everything is 'figuroutable'. I once worked with a business owner who was feeling tremendous overwhelm. We were joking around one day when she used the analogy that you don't eat a whole steer at once, you do it a bite at a time. (Sorry to you vegans or vegetarians out there, I am from Nebraska you know.) She got over her overwhelm by telling herself that she is smart and that there are resources that can help us achieve anything. In the day and age of YouTube and the internet, everything truly is 'figuroutable'.

This thought stuck with me. We set big goals and then want everything done now. At once. Immediately. And when it doesn't happen, we start to compare ourselves to others.

As Brené Brown once said, and for the life of me, I can't remember where, "Stay in your own lane." As the swimmer that she is, the advice was about swimming the absolute best you can without worrying about what others are doing. Not only can comparison kill creativity and joy, it can absolutely sabotage our self-worth and keep us from putting our best out into the world. When your sense of satisfaction is derived from comparing yourself to others, you are no longer the master of your own happiness.

Stay in your lane. When you feel good about something that you've done, don't allow anyone's opinions or accomplishments take that away from you.

Here is how comparison has stopped me before. For reference, this happened over 26 years ago and the memory still stays with me. When my husband I were getting ready for our wedding, we went through the traditional "convert to Catholicism" classes. During one of the first sessions, we met another young couple. The gal was a physician's assistant. She and my husband hit it off. They were discussing school and where they went. Here I was a college drop out. I immediately felt out of place. I didn't join in the conversation, which is so unlike me. The thoughts I had of myself (and her) plus the way I acted from the comparison going on in my mind still embarrasses me to this day. I never want to put myself out in the world like that again.

Was I mean? No. Did I act a bit rude for my own standards? Yes. Do I ever want to leave a conversation making anyone feeling less-than? Absolutely not.

It was a great lesson to learn about the power of the mind and what happens when we compare ourselves to others.

Another instance is in getting my business going. There are many times that I look at other people I follow and think I will never get as far as them. Or that I will never be as successful. That I should be further along in my journey than I am at this point.

While some people use this for motivation to go faster and work harder, it doesn't work for me. Because it does wreck my creativity. Comparison for motivation is okay if you know exactly what you are supposed to do, how you are supposed to do it and what winning looks like. Say for instance in basketball. There is a reason for a scoreboard. However, I would still argue that the more basketball players focus on others from a comparison standpoint, the worse off they are.

But in most of our lives, winning is not playing a sport. We don't score ourselves the same way as our peers. There are no hard and fast rules. There is no one at the end giving us a trophy or telling us how to get an A that is because we are unique individuals on our own journeys.

We are the ones that get to determine what success looks like. For that very reason, stop the comparisons!

Everything is figuroutable. Eat the cow one bite at a time.

> **Key takeaway:**
>
> Stop the comparisons and give yourself a break.

Chapter Sixteen

TIP: The Excuse Clause

Success is what comes after you stop making excuses. Or at the very least, get them out of the way.

All of this thought work may seem unattainable at times. So, how can we make it easier to see what we want? To ask for it? To ban the fear? To say, I am enough. I am ready. I truly don't care what others will think.

Here's a tool that has come in handy for me more than once. I like to call it the excuse clause. A few years ago, I had a leadership retreat for a board of directors. It was at a golf course and lodge and there were members of administration that were going to golf as well as some of the physicians and other board members. I like to golf and I really wanted to see this course as it is in the Sand Hills of Nebraska plus it is supposed to be difficult to play. For about ten days prior to the event, I kept contemplating canceling. I mean who was I after all to be golfing with people who I just knew were much, much, MUCH better than me. I was going to make a fool of myself I was sure. As each day inched closer, my ego kept screaming at me to send the message, send the message, for the love of Peter, Paul and Mary, send the darn message. You cannot golf with these people! What are you thinking! WE MAY DIE! But the intentional part of my brain knew that in order to grow as a person, I needed to keep what was truly starting to look like my appointment with disaster.

Upon arriving at the course, I found the CNO (Chief Nursing Officer) I was to golf with and suddenly got diarrhea of the mouth. I started talking as fast as my lips could carry the words. "I have only golfed twice this year and when I golf I go with my girlfriends and we only play nine holes, I'm not even sure I can finish 18 and we NEVER keep score!" To which she looked at me, smiled and replied, "Great, you have gotten all of your excuses out of the way!"

And you know what, it worked! So, get those excuses out of the way. State them, out loud if you need to, but whatever you do, don't let them hold you back.

> **Key takeaway:**
>
> List out all of your excuses and then do it anyway.

Chapter Seventeen

TIP: Learning to see other people's perspectives

There's my side of the story, my husband's side of the story and then there is what really happened.

Being able to see other people's perspectives can truly help us stay neutral. This in turn nixes the emotional drama that is such a time-suck. There is a great exercise I have used, coming from the book *Fierce Conversations,* for looking at perspectives and finding a different truth to what you believe.[13]

Imagine you are in a team meeting and you are standing on a stripe of a beach ball. All you can see from any viewpoint on your stripe is the color blue. A team member is standing on their stripe and all they can see is the color red. And yet a third member is on yellow and they will argue with you until the cows come home that the correct color of the ball is yellow. This is how you can begin to see the other sides or perspectives of any situation or story.

I read a great quote to this effect that states there are three sides to every story: yours, mine and what truly happened.

As a patient advocate who had to act like an investigator to recreate a complaint, I can tell you that there are usually more than three

---

[13] Scott, S. (2017). *Fierce conversations: Achieving success at work & in life, one conversation at a time.* London: Piatkus.

sides to any story. It just depends on how many people took part in the story. So, ask yourself:

Is my belief THE truth or just A truth - a perspective as I see if from my particular stripe on the beach ball?

What is the meaning I am giving that truth?

What feelings am I attaching to that truth?

To show you how this works, think about rain. What is the meaning you give rain? Think about it. If you are bride-to-be who has been planning the last 18 months for an outdoor wedding, rain will suck. If you are an artist with very expensive paintings at an outdoor art show, rain will really suck. If you are a farmer, who desperately needs the rain for his crops to grow, rain is glorious.

Do you understand how you assign meaning and feelings to situations? When those situations involve others and you are forming opinions of them, do you understand the meanings they are assigning to the conversation as well? Your beliefs determine what you do & feel. Therefore, you create your life because you are the interpreter. The belief creator. And it all starts with perspective.

> **Key takeaway:**
>
> To see other people's perspectives, think of living on a beach ball.

Chapter Eighteen

TIP: New habits, New responses

Bad habits are easier to abandon today than tomorrow.

~ Proverb

Habits can take time to build. Especially when it comes to our thinking. Think of it like a river. Your thoughts have been flowing down the same river since you were born. That is until something new, exciting, scary, or big happened. This flooded your river and possibly made a new offshoot stream. Once in a while some thought comes along that reminds you, "Hey! I have had this thought before." And your mind finds that stream.

Pretty soon, you get used to thinking that way and your brain finds the stream easier and easier until it to is a pretty smooth flowing river. This is all well and good until you decide, on purpose, to create a new stream. It will take conscious effort to pave the new stream and send water through it because quite honestly it is easier to send water down the old way. But you know it is worth it so you don't give up. And sooner or later, the stream will start to wear down its path and you will unconsciously start to pick it.

To get to that point, you truly have to engage your prefrontal cortex, that area of the brain that is required for conscious thought. According to research, we truly only have conscious thoughts about 5% of the time.[14] The rest of the time, our bodies are consumed with unconscious thoughts such as breathing and keeping our heart beating and semi-conscious thoughts like alerting us to needing to use the restroom.

Think about riding a bicycle. You had to concentrate like mad when you first were trying to ride. It is a lot of work trying to pedal and steer and watch the road and keep your balance all at once. So many things to think about and get in sync. But the saying "it's just like riding a bike" has stuck around for a reason. It's because once you expend all of the mental energy and teach your body how to do it, it is so easy to remember and pick back up.

What's more, once your brain has it hardwired in that manner, it is extremely difficult (as in oh-my-gosh I will never be able to change this habit) to try and rewire. Especially for adults. Destin Sandlin from Smarter Every Day did a cool experiment where he put the handlebars on a bike backwards and tried to retrain his mind and body to ride the bike.[15]

What took him 8 months of daily training to accomplish, his son was able to do in only 2 weeks. This is due to the neuroplasticity of our brains and how they build those super highways. What is cool about this is Destin talks about how little distractions such as his cell phone ringing sent his brain right back into the old way of doing things.

New habits are the same way. They can be a mind trick for a while. Remember Susan, the ICU nurse who worked her way up to senior director. Her habit was to jump in and fix the problem. She knew that in order to get out of her busyness mess, she needed to delegate

---

[14] Lipton, B. H. (2016). *The biology of belief: Unleashing the power of consciousness, matter & miracles.* Carlsbad, CA: Hay House.
[15] Sandlin, D. (Apr. 24, 2015) Smarter Every Day. *https://www.youtube.com/watch?v=MFzDaBzBlL0*

and let people 'make it or break it.' As you know, this is so much easier said than done.

We think things like, "It'll just be quicker if I go do it myself." Or "If I want it done right, I need to do it myself."

But these thoughts keep you in the weeds. As I mentioned earlier, this is THE biggest mindset shift for any manager or leader. So how do you keep yourself from sliding repeatedly back into those thoughts? The thoughts that ultimately create our actions?

You start to pave that stream. You consciously focus on the new thought and then you practice it. When Susan came to me, elated that she had told her charge nurse to handle the situation, she was paving her new stream.

It seems so easy, but watch your mind in action. When learning from Brooke about the model, she has you explore your thoughts and practice the model every single day. This is so that we can start to become the detective and see when our thoughts create a backslide in our behaviors.

Here is an easier example for you. I recently purchased my very own Glamper. While glamping is supposed to be fun and glamorous, this camper is definitely not the latter. It is a 1972 Kayot run-down canned ham type of camper. I was ecstatic the day I purchased it from a coworker. That was until I got in and started tearing out some of the rot. For some reason it didn't feel as simple as the DIY shows, blogs and articles had lead me to believe. It was 93 degrees and humid. I had sweat pouring into and out of places I don't even want to mention. The avocado and orange linoleum was peeling up, the refrigerator wasn't a fridge at all, some dude had put in a now defunct stereo system with wires and speakers messing up my soon to be glamour spot...It was a wreck!!!

My mind started to panic. The thoughts started rushing in, "Oh, no! I've gotten in over my head!"

"My husband is right. What was I thinking!"

"Who am I to think I can do this?"

"This is a disaster."

"I'm a failure."

Do these thoughts look or sound familiar to you? Have you ever quizzed yourself about a decision you made by asking, "What was I thinking?"

This is a dangerous thought because we usually never have our backs when our mind shouts this thought at us. Instead we start back pedaling - hard. And it almost always becomes personal.

We go from "This isn't working." To "I'm a failure" in the matter of seconds. This is the classic overwhelm game in action and is a signal that the imposter syndrome is at play.

It is this type of thinking that can keep us in busyness. It is far easier to think about and do what we have always done rather than intentionally work on thinking a new (seemingly harder) thought and practice it.

But here's the thing my friends, the more you do it - the easier it gets.

The more you do it - the more resilient you will become.

The more you do it - the faster you will be at getting out of stinkin thinkin!

Like everything else in life that is worthwhile (according to my parents) it will take some practice and hard work. But just like riding that bike, it will get easier and easier. I promise.

So, you will need to plan for the bad times. The crucial conversations are like dieting and dealing with the raging hunger or a case of the snackies. Focus on you – it is your path to happiness. Look for your triggers and remember there is a gap. Find your gap in thought and use your new response.

One secret I use is talking to myself. Or more accurately the part of me that is that inner critic. I tell my ego it will be okay. That whatever I am trying to do won't kill me and that no matter what I will keep taking steps forward. I use this mantra to remind me that by knowing my fear, I will learn how to move through it.

Move from No Fear to Know Fear.

What is your fear trying to tell you? Explore it and listen. Remember that sharing fear releases it. We need this because denial of fear means we buffer. We buffer by over eating, over drinking, gossiping and many other vices and habits in order to hide from our emotions. We usually aren't afraid of the action itself, but rather the judgments of the people. What's worse is that we actually judge the fear too by thinking we should know better or be better. Sometimes the best course of action is to just live with your thoughts and sit with them. Do nothing.

Then remember:

Are you being real with yourself?

Are you noticing the good as well as the bad?

Would you be this critical with your best friend?

And then ask yourself how would you support them? Do the same for yourself.

As for my little glamper (I can't decide if her name is Melba or Mabel), she is coming along just fine. I have taught myself things along the way that are harder than I thought. The process is definitely not glamorous, but it is oh-so rewarding. Check out my website to see the progress I am making at *kathybourque.com/glamper*

> **Key takeaway:**
>
> From the very profound Dori - "Just keep swimming."

Chapter Nineteen

TIP: *Show up and go bold.*

People are like stained-glass windows. They sparkle and shine when the sun is out, but when the darkness sets in, their true beauty is revealed only if there is a light from within.

~ Dr. Elisabeth Kübler-Ross

My hope for you is that this book has caused you to pause and look inside. For this is the true way we will all come to grips with our busy hectic lives and create better balance. By being true to who you are, you will soon realize that everything is happening just the way it is supposed to. When we aren't authentic we end up selling out on ourselves and other people.

Authenticity is beyond honesty.

~ Mike Robbins

Our super power is authenticity. It liberates us and touches and inspires those around us. It is what helps us glow like a beautiful stained-glass window.

My challenge to you is to build in moments of awareness. Check in with your perceptions, your beliefs, your story. Use these tools, this guidebook, to be true to you. To be remarkable. To shine from within. Remember that

nothing has meaning and that nobody is keeping a scorecard on your life but you.

Choose yourself. It's the external manifestation of if you better yourself, you better the lives of the people around you.

Effectiveness comes from being intentional. Intentionality comes from knowing ourselves and being true to that. To stop wasting time caring about what others think. And to put your best foot forward in a way that only you can do. Practice is necessary. But it is all so worth it.

Always remember this:

The world doesn't need your self-imposed limitations, your fear."

~ Cory Bookers Dad

It doesn't need you to play small. The world needs you to show up and to go bold.

References

https://www.gallup.com/workplace/237059/employee-burnout-part-main-causes.aspx

https://hbr.org/2000/09/why-should-anyone-be-led-by-you

http://www.kathybourque.com/busyness-workbook

https://www.mindtools.com/pages/article/newTMC_5W.htm

http://www.drcloud.com/

https://jamesclear.com/willpower-decision-fatigue

http://www.kathybourque.com/core-values

https://www.thelifecoachschool.com/podcasts/

http://www.thework.com/en/do-work

http://www.10percenthappier.com/mindfulness-meditation-the-basics/

https://www.inc.com/jim-schleckser/the-70-rule-when-to-delegate.html

https://www.youtube.com/watch?v=MFzDaBzBlL0

http://www.kathybourque.com/glamper

http://www.thebodysoulconnection.com/EducationCenter/previous.html

About the Author

KATHY BOURQUE

Growing up in Illinois as the oldest of four girls, Kathy learned how to be a people pleasing perfectionist. This trait seemed to serve her well until she years later when she started asking the big questions we all seem to face in life, such as "Who am I and what is my purpose?"

After years of self-exploration, leadership development and graduating from the school of hard knocks, Kathy now teaches others how to combat that people-pleasing-perfectionist personality to show up and be effective as leaders.

Kathy believes that we are all leaders because leadership is influence. But before leading others, we need to be able to lead ourselves and managing our minds is the only way to do this.

Kathy is a non-traditional student in every sense of the term. She finished her bachelor's degree 30 years after she started and went on to get her Master of Science in Leadership and Management. She considers herself a consummate explorer and loves to travel.

Between speaking and doing workshops, as well as work for a hospital foundation, Kathy currently resides in Nebraska with her husband, son and dog Lucky.

kathybourque.com

@kathybourque

www.ingramcontent.com/pod-product-compliance
Lightning Source LLC
Chambersburg PA
CBHW030649220526
45463CB00005B/1699